Sweet Slices of History

Sweet Slices of History

Marjory Szurko

PROSPECT BOOKS
2018

This edition published in 2018 in Great Britain and the USA by Prospect Books at 26 Parke Road, London, SW13 9NG.

Text © 2018 Marjory Szurko.
Illustrations by Tim Kirtley.

British Library Cataloguing in Publication Data:
A catalogue entry for this book is available from the British Library.

ISBN 978-1-909248-60-1

Set in Adobe Garamond Pro and Cochin by Catheryn Kilgarriff and Brendan King.

Printed by the Gutenberg Press Ltd., Malta.

Contents

Contents

INTRODUCTION

I have loved cookery from my earliest childhood. I was born into a close-knit family in a Georgian house on the outskirts of Glasgow, where my father was the young principal of a theological college. My mother was a trained cook who gave the college community their meals, and taught rudimentary culinary skills to many of the students so that they could manage on a slender salary during the post-war years. I remember happy days in the kitchen as a child, sitting on the floor with my back against the warmth of the Aga cooker, eating rhubarb gathered from the garden, and watching my mother dash around the kitchen, straining pots of crab-apple jelly on the deep window sills or making bread on the huge wooden table.

After studying English Language and Literature, I trained to be a librarian, and when I took up the post of librarian at Oriel College Oxford in 2002, my dual interests of librarianship and cookery came together.

Amidst a large number of fine volumes which an alumnus named Stephen Noel Furness had bequeathed to Oriel library on his death in 1974, I discovered a small recipe book entitled the *Otterington Hall Recipe Book*. The book had been compiled and edited by Stephen Furness and his sister Mary, from the recipes of their mother and her guests over many years in their country house in Yorkshire.

I was particularly inspired by the introduction, which read: 'We hope that the Recipes may be enjoyable to others but we hope too that they will, if only for a brief moment, bring back memories of days which now appear so golden – of Mother active and astir in the garden whilst we younger people were still getting up, of old friends and young friends seated around her table…so much fun and happiness of which she was the source and centre – these things still come back to us across the years.'[1]

When I read this, I realized that it might be possible to recreate the kind of atmosphere described in the book by baking and serving some of the sweet dishes in college. After receiving the permission of the Furness family, I made up some of the recipes and circulated instructions for others which were tasty, attractive to the eye, and appropriate as 'finger food'. To my delight, many of the Staff and Fellows of the College joined with me to contribute baked goods made in their own kitchens.

The event was named an 'Edible Exhibition', and the first one was held in the Small Senior Common Room at Oriel on 18 December 2002. This date was chosen because it would have been Stephen Furness' 100th birthday. The original recipes and their sources were presented on exhibition cards, while items from the Furness book collection were exhibited in the eighteenth century Senior Library above to accompany the feast.

This experiment, attended by the college community and friends around Oxford, was a great success, and I was encouraged to hold more in the years that followed. As I had a fair knowledge of Middle English, I decided to try some recipes from the fourteenth century, the century in which Oriel College was founded. Although there were no more cookery books in the library at Oriel, I collected modern transcriptions of such works as the fourteenth century *Curye on Inglysch*[2] (where the word 'curye' is taken from the Middle French word *cuire* meaning 'to cook') and *Two Fifteenth-Century Cookery-Books*[3] and was able to examine manuscript cookery texts in other Oxford libraries and archives, plundering them for sweet recipes.

The recipes that have come down to us from early centuries were from courts, or from noble households, as those were the households of people who could afford to buy the ingredients, and employ chefs who could read, write, and record the recipes.

I found when I started baking the early recipes myself that it was one thing to translate them, but another thing entirely to make them work. Even when they were translated, the fact remained that the recipes were not easy to understand or to put into modern terminology. There were no lists of ingredients – these were included as part of the general text. The measurements were basic; temperatures were not indicated; quantities were not often specified, and timing was vague. It was assumed that the person reading the recipes would have some knowledge of cooking.

The first early recipe I attempted to make was 'payn ragoun', a honey and pine-nut sweet from *Curye on Inglysch* (IV, 68). On reading it over, I saw that it involved heating sugar and honey together, but the only instructions relating to temperature were '…with esy fyre, and kepe it wel fro brenning…' I took 'esy fyre' to mean 'on a low heat', so that I could keep the sugar and honey mixture from burning in the pan ('kepe it wel fro brynning').

The next part of the recipe gave me heart, because it resembled instructions that my mother had given me when I was a young girl learning to make toffee: 'And whan it hath yboiled a while, take vp a drope þerof wiþ þy fyngur and do it in a litel water, and loke if it hong togydre...' While I was reading this, it dawned on me that it was the 'soft ball' test for boiled sugar, in which you drop a small quantity of the mixture into cold water and gather it between your finger and thumb to see if it is ready; a test that you can do even now if you don't have a sugar thermometer! In my mind's eye, I could see the illustration of the process that my mother had pointed out in the cookery book we were using, and this gave me comfort and confidence that I was working along the right lines. One of the things I learned from this first experiment was that modern recipes have their roots in these old recipes of the past, and that I might be able to understand the instructions more easily than I had thought at first.

Increasingly, historic food has become a subject for scholars to study at undergraduate and postgraduate level, and the Edible Exhibitions have provided an opportunity for other people to share in the making of the dishes, as well as in the sampling of them, teaching participants and guests alike how the food of earlier times would have tasted, and more importantly, how the particular combination of flavours would work in practice. There is no substitute for *creating* the dishes rather than simply reading the recipes – in this way, you can find the pitfalls, rectify your errors, and experience the triumph of making the product, with the taste as the reward.

One thing that struck guests when they sampled medieval-style food for the first time was that it was rich, subtle, and spicy. They were expecting the food to be very bland and basic, but were pleasantly surprised to find that intricate flavours and unexpected ingredients combined to deliver an exciting taste.

The explanation for the inclusion of spices in medieval food was that after the eleventh century, there was a great deal of travelling to

Some of the recipe books and ingredients that inspired the Edible Exhibitions.

and from the crusades, which lasted into the fourteenth century, and spices were discovered and were then imported from the east and from Europe, as people found that they liked them. The cheapest imported spices were pepper and ginger. Cinnamon was very highly priced, but was used often. Before the eighteenth century, sugar was an extremely expensive commodity, and came in 'loaves' from which the sugar was cut off as needed. Honey was used rather than sugar by most people as a sweetener, and in some medieval recipes sugar was suggested only if it was affordable. The most expensive spice of all (costly even today) was saffron, which comes from the stamens of crocuses. Saffron was grown widely for a while in places such as Saffron Walden, but supply could not keep up with demand, so it was usually imported from Spain, which is also the case today.

Table of food laid out at one of the Edible Exhibitions.

The Edible Exhibitions were certainly valuable from a culinary point of view, but they also provided a social focus reminiscent of the French salons of the eighteenth and nineteenth centuries, bringing together students, staff, librarians, tutors, faculty members, professors, and friends from different parts of Oxford society who may never have met otherwise. With the common talking points of food, drink, and literary objects, the people who flocked to these gatherings were able to discuss every subject under the sun in a relaxed atmosphere, with no pressure of any kind to mar their enjoyment of each other and the food.

Sweet Slices of History is the story of how I located and chose the recipes I did, from the royal court and the mysterious halls of Oxford in the fourteenth century to the country house kitchen in the nineteenth and early twentieth centuries, all brought to life as sweet feasts on today's table. I will let you into the secrets of the recipes themselves, and let them speak to you as they have done to me.

CHAPTER ONE

COURTLY CUISINE

FOURTEENTH CENTURY

The first 'Edible Exhibition' at Oriel College really did produce the warm atmosphere that Stephen and Mary Furness had described in the preface to the *Otterington Hall Recipe Book*. This was the result of hospitality, entertainment, good company, conversation with friends and colleagues, the excitement of eating the food we had made together, and the discussion of the books on show. The festive afternoon inspired me to think about other events that I could host along the same lines, and although I was encouraged in this by many members of Oriel, I had no idea of what could follow it until a chance gift I received put an idea into my head.

Several people who had enjoyed that first feast gave me gifts of various recipe books that they had come across. One of the books that I received in this way was the Early English Text Society edition of *Two Fifteenth-Century Cookery-Books* edited by Thomas Austin, which I looked through with interest. I noticed that there was an abundance of meat dishes, and that many familiar spices such as cinnamon, pepper, ginger, and saffron were used throughout. This first glance intrigued me.

I realized I had no clear idea of what cooking and eating would have been like in early centuries, and since Oriel College had been founded in 1326, I was curious to know what kind of food the Oriel founders and scholars would have enjoyed. The first scholars of Oriel College received their foundation charter from King Edward II in 1326, and lodged in Tackley's Inn, a large hall which can still be seen within Oriel, behind the shops on Oxford's High Street. What food would they have eaten? What influenced their cooking? I was eager to find out!

The first thing I felt I should do was to gather information about early English cookery, and running through my mind was the advice I had learned long ago: 'Start from where you are!' As I was Librarian at Oriel, I looked in the library there to find any books on the food of the past which would be helpful to read. The great advantage of having access to such a collection is that interesting and varied books have been presented to the library over the centuries by generous benefactors, so there are many to be found on almost all subjects.

The main book that I found to help me was entitled *The Delectable Past*, by Esther B. Aresty. It had been given by a history tutor from the 1960s, William Abel Pantin (or Billy Pantin, as he was widely known). It would have been newly published when Dr Pantin purchased it.

The author had been an avid book collector, particularly interested in early cookbooks. She first describes one of the oldest books in her collection, an ancient Greek work entitled *The Deipnosophists*, where various foods of the day were described, including fish dishes of all kinds, and cheesecakes, which were made mostly on the island of Samos, known as the cheesecake-making island.[1] I had imagined that the cheesecake was a modern food, but here it was mentioned in an ancient text!

Aresty then tells us about the earliest Roman cookbook *De re coquinaria*, or *De re culinaria* as it is sometimes known. Translated, the title means 'On culinary matters'. This cookbook was probably penned in the eighth or ninth century AD, and may have been written by a Roman gourmet called Apicius. The recipes in the book, we are told, were little more than a list of ingredients: 'The style of cooking ran to heavy spicing, and meats combined with sweet syrups or with honey and vinegar. The recipes make strange reading until one recognizes that many sweet-and-sour dishes enjoyed today are roundabout descendants of this same Apician cookery.'[2]

Aresty goes on to say that *De re coquinaria* was in use until at least the fifteenth century. She knew this because she had a hand-written copy of the work in her possession which had been made around the year 1400.

The author then mentions an English cookbook known as *The Forme of Cury*, compiled by the cooks who served Richard II, and written at the end of the century. The word 'cury' comes from the French *cuire* ('to cook'), and the title means 'method of cooking'. Aresty gives the recipes for 'salat' (a dish of herbs) and 'Mawmenny' (a capon stew) from the book, and mentions that these dishes are also distinguished by their heavy spicing, as were the Roman recipes which preceded them. I have discovered that Esther Aresty gave her collection of cookbooks to the University of Pennsylvania when she died in 2000, and they are available to be seen there.

Looking at *The Delectable Past* convinced me that it was worth trying to bake early sweet recipes if I could get hold of them. This thought coincided with the encouragement of Dr Jeremy Catto, one of Oriel's medieval historians, who knew that I had studied Old and Middle English in university, and was sure that I was capable of putting on an Edible Exhibition from fourteenth-century recipes. I must admit that I was rather intimidated by the thought of making these recipes at first, because I felt that my translation could led me astray, and I wondered if the flavours and tastes would translate to modern expectations of food, but Dr Catto also gave me a little book entitled *To the King's Taste: Richard II's Book of Feasts and Recipes Adapted for Modern Cooking* by Lorna Sass to show me how it could be done. Added to this, there were two English tutors at Oriel who knew Middle English: Dr Glenn Black and Dr James Methven. They not only helped me with the translations, but were talented bakers themselves, who were happy to experiment along with me to find out if modern kitchens and ingredients could replicate the originals. I decided that I could look in modern recipe books to find out if there were any equivalent recipes that would help me work out the amount of each ingredient to be used, and this did indeed give me the basis of many of the recipes I tried. Unfamiliar food in any guise, but particularly food from the past, can seem worryingly alien and unfamiliar, but once we get past these moments of hesitation, and gain confidence in the recipes and in our own abilities, we find that a new world of food opens up for us.

Two Fifteenth-Century Cookery-Books included two menus from the fourteenth century: those of a feast of three courses made for King

Richard II when he was dining with the Bishop of Durham in London on 23 September 1387,[3] and the three-course banquet for the coronation of King Henry IV in Westminster Hall in 1399.[4] I read through these menus so that I could have an idea of the type of sweet dishes that would have been present at a fourteenth-century feast.

When I studied the two menus, it was hard to decide which were the sweet dishes, as there were very few items in the menus that appeared to be in this category. I thought that 'Crustade lumbard in paste', 'Payne puff', 'Longe Frutours', 'Leche lumbarde', 'Frytourys', 'Doucettyes' and 'Pety perneux' all looked as if they could be desserts. Each of the courses on both menus ended with an item called a 'Sotelte' or 'Sotellte', described tantalisingly in the glossary and index as 'Subtlety, or device to deck the Table'.[5]

Flicking over the fifteenth century recipes for hints on how to make the dishes, I saw that several contained meat of various types. It dawned on me that the old word for desserts – 'sweetmeats' – a term still in use today, was accurate in this setting, although as I knew from my studies, the Middle English term 'mete' (originally meaning 'to measure, or mete out') did not necessarily mean 'meat' as we know it, but could just mean 'food'.

This in turn made me think of mince pies (or mincemeat tarts), a popular part of English Christmas fare today, which up until the later twentieth century regularly contained actual meat (usually mutton, beef, or veal, and suet or animal fat) as well as raisins, currants, and fruit peel. In my mother's kitchen nothing was thrown away if it could still be consumed – even now, my brother and I preserve little jars of fat or savoury jelly in the fridge to be used in future meals – and so it must have been in the medieval kitchen. Meat was hard to come by, and if it could be sweetened with spices, honey and sugar to preserve it, or cooked with fruit to give it flavour, it could be considered a dessert.

Many fruits and nuts would have been available locally in the fourteenth century for use in cooking and baking. Pine nuts grew in Britain, as did almonds (in fact I gathered almonds from my neighbour's tree as far north as Manchester when I was young), and apples and soft fruits were abundant. Exotic fruits and spices such as oranges, lemons, figs, dates and raisins were imported from Spain or the Orient.

Books give us a very incomplete picture of the food from earlier centuries, but they are often the only guides we have, apart from a few paintings that survive. In the thirteenth century, a didactic poem called 'The Treatise' by Walter of Bibbesworth, an English knight, describes the sweet dishes that come after a meal: 'And when the table was taken away, sweet spice powder with large dragees, maces, cubebs and enough spicerie and plenty of wafers'.[6] Dragees include sugared almonds, and the word comes originally from the Greek word *tragema* meaning sweet or nut treat, coming down to us from Old French *dragie*. Cubebs were dried berries originating in Java or Sumatra, and often sugared and served as an aromatic confection.

Modern food preferences, lifestyle choices, and even dietary requirements, mean meat is no longer an automatic preference for many people. I preferred the sweet dishes that I baked to have no meat in them because I wanted as many people as possible to be able to eat and enjoy the food provided. In medieval times most people kept to the Christian fast days, and those included Fridays (when people would eat fish rather than meat), and Lent (a fasting period of the Christian church just before Easter). These rules are still generally kept today in many parts of England. A choice of recipes was often offered to use on 'fisshe days' when only fish was allowed, as opposed to 'flesche days' when meat was eaten.

When I had familiarised myself with the fifteenth-century recipes, I went through the index of the other volumes in the series to see if there were more transcripts of recipe books from earlier centuries, and found *Curye on Inglysch: English Culinary Manuscripts of the Fourteenth Century (including The Forme of Cury)*, edited by Constance B. Hieatt and Sharon Butler, and published in 1985. So here was the original text of *The Forme of Cury* that I had first heard of in Esther Aresty's book – I couldn't wait to read it. I got hold of a copy of it, and started thinking about translating some of the recipes for sweet dishes found in it.

Although it is well known that bread and salt were the earliest form of hospitality given to strangers, there didn't seem to be any recipes for bread in the cookbooks I looked at from the fourteenth century. Cultivated yeast as we know it had not been invented, so the bakers would have used natural yeast occurring in ale and beer barm (the froth that forms on the top of fermenting malt liquors) to make their bread rise. This would most likely have been in the form of sourdough bread. Bread was obviously plentiful, as it was used for stuffing in many recipes, and the writers refer to 'payndemayn' or 'wastel bread' which was best quality white bread, and sometimes 'manchet' which was also of a good quality. Hieatt and Butler note in the index to *Curye on Inglysch* that 'payndemayn' had been thought to derive from *panis dominis* 'lord's bread', but some medieval sources suggest that the best quality flour was called 'mayne' and so the best bread was that which was made out of mayne flour. This could also apply to 'manchet', combining 'mayne' and 'cheat', meaning 'loaf'.[7]

I started my experiments with 'payn ragoun' from *The Forme of Cury*, as the ingredients informed me that this really was a sweet dish. I thought at first glance that it might be something to do with bread (from the French word *pain*), but there didn't seem to be any bread in it at all, although the pine nuts were a substitute, acting like breadcrumbs to bulk up the ingredients. I practised making the payn ragoun, adjusting the recipe as I went, giving tasters to my husband and various friends until I was satisfied with the result. None of my 'guinea-pigs' complained!

PAYN RAGOUN

Take hony and sugur cipre and clarifie it togydre, and boile it with esy fyre, and kepe it wel fro brennyng. And whan it hath yboiled a while, take vp a drope thereof wiþ þy fyngur and do it in a litel water, and loke if it hong togydre; and take it fro the fyre and do þereto pynes the thriddendele & powdour gyngeuer, and stere it togyder til it bigynne to thik, and caste it on a wete table; lesh it and serue it forth with fryed mete, on flesh dayes or on fysshe dayes.[8]

[Translation: Take honey and Cyprian sugar and clarify them

together, and boil it on a low fire, and [by all means] keep it from burning. When it has boiled a while, take up a drop of it with your finger and put it in a little [cold] water, and observe if it hangs together; and take it from the fire and put the third part of pine nuts into it and powdered ginger, and stir it together until it begins to thicken, and put it on a wet table; slice it and serve it with fried meat, on flesh days or on fish days.]

Ingredients:
450 g / 16 oz / 2 cups caster sugar (1 cup = 8 oz)
3 tbpns clear honey
125 ml / 4 fl oz / ½ cup water
¾ to 1 cup pine nut kernels, chopped small or ground
1 rounded tsp ground ginger

Method: Put the sugar, honey and water in a deep pan and cook over low heat until a sugar thermometer placed in it registers 110 °C / 230 °F. At once, turn the syrup into a chilled bowl and beat it hard for 2-3 minutes; then beat in the remaining ingredients.

Turn the mixture into a wetted shallow pan (or cover the pan with non-stick paper) and leave to harden. The name of the dish ('payn') suggests it is to be seen as a type of bread, so you can slice it as you would a loaf, but I found it easier and more attractive to cut it into fairly small pieces to serve (more like pieces of fudge or Scottish tablet). You could also roll it into balls and coat the balls in ginger or cinnamon to serve.

Notes: The first batch of these I tried were too sticky, so I added ½ cup of water, as in other toffee recipes I had tried in the past, and that helped the mixture, although it was not in the original recipe.

The directions in the recipe seem to call for it to be made up by using enough pine nuts to make up a third of the mixture, so I did that here (the term 'thriddendele' is not clear). I also chopped the pine nuts, to be more like the breadcrumb thickener that appears in other medieval recipes, although again, this direction was not in the original recipe. This is a good first recipe for you to try, just as I did, so that you can get a feel for medieval cookery. Feel free to experiment with the pine nuts as I did to find the consistency that you like best.

The next recipe I tried was 'pety pervant' because it had been in one of the fourteenth-century menus (as 'pety perneux'), and I felt that if I could make a basic medieval pastry using the instructions in it, I could make other pies and tarts according to medieval methods, and then distribute the recipe to others who wanted to make pastry dishes.

When I looked more closely at the instructions in the recipe, I had second thoughts about the nature of this pastry. I had been making shortcrust pastry for years, and all the recipes I had used relied on very cold water to make them work, but the recipe for 'pety pervant' definitely instructed the cook not to let water come anywhere near it. Instead, I made up a recipe for pastry that used vegetable oil and egg yolks instead of water, and it seemed to work well enough.

PETY PERUAUNT

Take male marrow hole parade, and kerue it rawe; powdour of ginger, sugur, ʒolkes of ayren, dates minced, raisouns of coraunce, salt, a lytel, & loke þat þou make þy past with ʒolkes of ayren & þat no water come þerto; and fourme þy coffin and make up þy past.[9]

[Translation: Petty pervant (from the French *petit provaunt*, meaning 'small provisions').[10] Take marrow [from a marrow-bone] pared whole from the bone, and carve it raw; powdered ginger, sugar, yolks of eggs, minced dates, raisins of Corinth (i.e. currants), a little salt, and be careful that you make your pastry with yolks of eggs and that no water comes into it, and form your case and make up your pastry.]

Ingredients for pastry:
175 g / 6 oz / ¾ cup plain white flour
½ tsp salt

½ tbsp sugar
2 egg yolks (beaten)
2 tbsps vegetable oil

Method for pastry: Sift together flour and salt in a large bowl. Mix sugar, egg yolks and vegetable oil in a small bowl, then quickly stir into flour mixture and knead into a soft, pliable dough, using more flour if necessary.

Cover the dough with a tea towel and leave it to one side while the filling is prepared. To make up, roll out the dough with a rolling pin to fit into the bottom and sides of an 18 cm / 7 in flan dish.

Ingredients for filling:
1 tsp ground ginger
2 tbsps brown sugar
1 tbsp marrowbone fat or lard or butter
2 egg yolks
10-12 dates without stones, cut into small pieces
½ cup of currants
pinch of salt

Method for filling: Line the pie/tart cases with dried fruits. Combine remaining ingredients in a bowl. Beat until thoroughly blended. Pour over fruits in the cases. Bake at 190 °C / 375 °F / gas mark 5 for 15-20 minutes or until the top is set and light brown. Cool before serving.

Notes: It is difficult to know what kind of pastry was used for this dish, as pastry making does not seem to be described thoroughly in any of the recipes of the time. This may be because it was so familiar to medieval cooks that they didn't bother to record the method, or because the recipes were made by cooks rather than bakers.

If you want the dish to be vegetarian, use butter throughout, but if you'd rather experience what it would really have tasted like, ask a butcher to cut out some marrowbone fat for you, and use that. The result is a savoury fruit tart that melts in your mouth.

Reading through the many different recipes for fritters, my attention was drawn to 'Frytour of pasternaks, of skyrwittes, & of apples'. None of us had heard of 'skyrwittes' and when I looked them up in the index, it mentioned that John Gerard, the sixteenth-century herbalist, had said that they resembled parsnips. We all thought some apple fritters would be popular, and we also wanted to try parsnip fritters as they would be unusual. I looked in some of my daily cookbooks to find that the recipes for making fritters had not changed very much over the years, and I was also guided by Lorna Sass' interpretations.[11] The fritters would be far better made hot, but I lived out of college so had the difficulty of not having an oven close by. Fortunately, the Dean of the College at the time, Dr James Methven, offered to make the apple fritters on site, and very good they were too! He ran over from time to time to supply the waiting crowd with a few hot spicy apple fritters and tender delicate parsnip fritters just off the stove – delicious!

Frytour of Pasternaks, of Skyrwittes, & of Apples

Take skyrwittes and pasternakes and apples & perboile hem. Make a batour of flour and ayren; cast þerto ale & ʒest, safroun & salt. Wete hem in þe batour, and frye hem in oile or in grece; do þerto aulmand mylke, & serue it forth.[12]

[Translation: Take skirrets and parsnips and apples and parboil them. Make a batter of flour and eggs and add some ale and barm (yeast), saffron and salt. Dip them in the batter, and fry them in oil or grease; serve with almond milk.]

Batter:
225 g / 8 oz / 1 cup plain flour
½ tsp salt
½ tsp saffron
2 eggs (separated)
225 ml / 8 fl oz / 1 cup warm ale
100 ml / 4 fl oz / ½ cup milk

Sieve flour and salt, beat in egg yolks, ale, milk and saffron. Finally fold in stiffly beaten egg whites to add volume. The batter will be thick and fairly smooth. Leave it to stand for about 15 minutes for the saffron to colour it.

Apple Fritters

6 large firm apples
175 g / 6 oz / ¾ cup lard or 6 tbsps vegetable oil
1 tbsp sugar

Method: Peel and core the apples and cut them into slices 6 mm / ¼ in thick. Dust slices with flour added to half of the sugar to help the batter adhere, and then dip slices into the batter. Fry in hot oil until both sides are golden brown. Drain on absorbent paper. Sprinkle the rest of the sugar over fritters through a sieve, and serve.

Apple fritters.

PARSNIP FRITTERS

12 medium parsnips
175 g / 6 oz / ¾ cup lard or 6 tbsps vegetable oil
salt to taste

Method: Scrape parsnips and cut in thirds lengthwise, then cut each section in half. Steam sections over boiling water for about 10 minutes, until they are tender. Drain on absorbent paper. Dip in batter and fry in hot oil until golden. Sprinkle with salt and serve.

Note: The fritter recipe, and many of the other recipes in those early centuries, included saffron, which had much to commend it to medieval cooks. Saffron was golden – a rich colour connected with royalty. Alchemy was also prevalent in the early centuries, and it was thought that it was possible to turn base metals into gold. Because of this idea, anything that was gold in colour was revered and thought to

Parsnip fritters.

have special magical qualities. People used to wear little bags containing saffron or marigolds around their necks to guard them from evil, and to give them good fortune.

After the experiment with the pastry for 'pety pervant', which did not include water, I decided to record my own everyday recipe for shortcrust pastry with the idea that we could regularly use this pastry for the base of the sweet dishes that would follow. I took ingredients which would have been found in medieval times to make up 'crusts' or 'coffins'.

There may have been two kinds of medieval pastry: a tough, inedible variety which would have been merely a holder for the ingredients of the dish, and a true pastry case that would have been part of the meal, but this cannot be proven, so I decided to make all the pastry edible.

Taking 8 ounces of flour to 4 ounces of butter, I could make pastry for at least one large uncovered pastry case or 12 tart cases, and any extra could be wrapped in foil to put in the freezer for up to three months. I have used this mixture in all the succeeding recipes which call for pastry, unless the recipe has specifically called for a different method or ingredients.

BASIC MEDIEVAL-STYLE SHORTCRUST PASTRY

Ingredients:
225 g / 8 oz / 1 cup plain white flour
110 g / 4 oz / ½ cup butter, or a mixture of half butter and half lard
1 tsp sugar
1 tsp salt
1 ½ tbsps very cold water
1 egg, beaten

Method: Take the butter/lard out of the refrigerator and leave at room temperature until it softens up a little, so that you can work with it, but don't leave it until it is too soft. Sift the flour, salt and sugar onto a pastry sheet or board, and then cut the butter/lard up into very small pieces and mix these with the flour until all the fat becomes coated with flour. Work by pinching the pieces of fat with your fingers and work quickly so that it remains as cool as possible.

When the fat is combined with the flour, pile the whole mixture into a mound, and make a hole in the centre to pour in the cold water and beaten egg. Stir this into the flour, then mix it with the heel of your hand until the dough becomes smooth. If the dough is too dry and crumbly, add ½ to 1 teaspoon of water. If it is too wet, add a little more flour. Work the dough for another 2-3 minutes until it is perfectly smooth.

Make the dough into a ball and divide it into the number of portions that you want, cutting small tarts from one portion of pastry. Wrap the portions in either greaseproof paper or plastic wrap and put it in the fridge for 1-2 hours before using it. The pastry will keep for at least two days in the refrigerator, and for at least two months in a freezer. You could also use a food processor, or a mixer with a dough hook to make your pastry. I used to be quite wary of making pastry, but this recipe seems to be a fail-safe one. You can substitute rosewater or orange water for some of the ordinary tap water in the original recipe, or even mix saffron strands into the pastry if the recipe calls for these.

The next recipes I looked at were two recipes for cheesecake. The first recipe was a simple Brie tart, using a semi-soft cheese known as 'ruayn' which was a bit softer than the kind of Brie we get today, so a young Brie is best to use, as Lorna Sass explains.[13]

You may be as surprised as I was to hear that Brie would be paired with ginger and saffron. Ginger has to be used very sparingly or it masks other tastes, and saffron is earthy and faintly flowery, so it bridges the gap between savoury and sweet, but if the ingredients are mixed well, with only a hint of ginger, the flavours complement each other. This works particularly well if the dish is accompanied by a sweet wine or punch, like the mulled wine 'Hippocras' which was drunk liberally at fourteenth-century feasts.

TART DE BRY

Take a crust ynche depe in a trap. Take 3olkes of ayren rawe and chese ruayn and medle it and the 3olkes together. And do thereto powdour gynger, sugar, safroun and salt. Do it in a trap, bake it, & serue it forth.[14]

[Translation: Brie tart. Make a pastry case an inch deep. Take raw yolks of eggs and semi-soft cheese and mix it and the yolks together. And add to it powdered ginger, sugar, saffron and salt. Put it in a case, bake it and serve it forth.]

Ingredients (serves 8-10):
Shortcrust pastry (see pages 27-8 for ingredients and method)
6 egg yolks, beaten
450 g / 1 lb Brie cheese
25 strands / ¼ tsp powdered saffron
¾ tsp light brown sugar
¼ tsp powdered ginger
¼ tsp salt

Tart de Bry (right foreground).

Method: Bake pastry case at 220 ºC / 425 ºF / gas mark 7, for 10 minutes, using baking beans or another method to stop the pastry from bubbling up in the oven. Put it in a very deep dish, so that it can be at least an inch deep, and don't trim the crust until after it has baked. While this is cooling, remove the rind from the Brie with a sharp knife. You can cut the rind into small pieces and sprinkle them evenly on the pie crust for a stronger flavour. If you are using saffron strands, rather than the powder, soak them in a few spoonfuls of hot water for five minutes over the heat first to bring the colour out. Mix the Brie with remaining ingredients using an egg beater or blender until it is as smooth as possible. Add salt to taste. Pour mixture into pastry case. Bake at 180 ºC / 350 ºF / gas mark 4, for 30 to 40 minutes or until set and brown on top.

Notes: If you use the young Brie rind, it gives a very tasty strong flavour, which is enriched by the saffron and ginger.

The following recipe for sambocade, or Elderflower cheesecake, was the star of the show as far as we were concerned. The teaspoonful of rosewater deepens the flavour of the cheese mixture into something rich and subtle, and gives it that never-to-be-forgotten faint fragrance of roses. Many of us had never before tasted a dish flavoured with rosewater, and most of us were captivated by it.

The name 'sambocade' is derived from the Latin word for elderflowers: *sambucus*. The elder has long been considered a mystical plant, and many medieval people thought it was able to ward off danger, and possessed healing powers. It is worth picking fresh elderflowers and drying them for this subtle dish rather than using cordial. I was fortunate – my brother had just gathered some elderflowers from the surrounding trees while they were flowering, dried them in bundles on the clothes pulley in his kitchen, and had given me some of those. They can keep for at least two months if kept dry and well wrapped. The flowers are also used in brewing, so they can be bought from brewing suppliers.

SAMBOCADE

*Take and make a crust in a trap & take cruddes and wryng out þe
wheyȝe and draw hem þurgh a straynour and put hit in þe crust. Do
þerto sugur the thridde part, & somdel whyte of ayren, & shake þerin
blomes of elren; & bake it vp with eurose & messe it forth.*[15]

[Translation: Make a pastry case and take curds and wring out the
whey and pass it through a strainer and put it in the case. Add the
third part of sugar, and some whites of eggs, and shake elderflowers
on it, and bake it with rosewater and serve it up.]

Ingredients (serves 8):
Shortcrust pastry (see pages 27-8 for ingredients and method)
3 tbsps dried elderflowers
4 tbsps double cream
125 g / 4 ½ oz / ⅓ cup sugar
225 g / ½ lb / 1 cup cottage cheese
225 g / ½ lb / 1 cup ricotta cheese
1 tbsp rosewater
6 egg whites, beaten until stiff but not dry

Method: Bake pastry case at 220 ºC / 425 ºF / gas mark 7, for 10 minutes.
Let it cool. Soak elderflowers in double cream for about 10 minutes.
Add sugar and stir until dissolved. Push cheeses through a strainer with
the back of a tablespoon. Combine cheeses with elderflower-cream
mixture and blend thoroughly. Fold in stiff egg whites. Pour mixture
into pastry crust. Bake at 190 ºC / 375 ºF / gas mark 5, for about 50
minutes or until firm but not dry. Turn off heat and allow to cool in the
oven with the door open for about 15 minutes.

When I saw a recipe for gingerbread in the compilation of writings
entitled *Goud Kokery*, in section V of *Curye on Inglysch*, I knew it had
to be part of the fourteenth-century feast. Ginger has always been a

popular spice, and its uses have been both culinary and medicinal through the ages, counteracting respiratory difficulties, helping weak stomachs, and 'balancing the humours', as well as adding to the taste of dishes in the kitchen.

There were two kinds of gingerbread in the fourteenth century, as the editors explain in the index of *Curye on Inglysch* – the toffee-like confection, which, according to the recipe is made to be 'as thick as wax', and pulled around a pin of wood or hartshorn to stretch it; or the cake-like variety made with breadcrumbs,[16] which is the one we chose to make.

GINGERBREDE

To make gingerbrede. Take goode honye & clarifie it on þe fere, & take fayre paynemayn or wastel brede & grate it, & caste it into þe boylenge hony, & stere it well togyder faste with a sklyse þat it bren not to þe vessell. & þanne take it doun and put þerin ginger, longe pepere & saundres, & tempere it vp with þin handes; & than put hem to a flatt boyste & strawe þeron suger, & pick þerin clowes rounde aboute by þe egge and in þe mydes, yf it plece you, &c.[17]

[Translation: Take good honey and clarify it on the fire, and take the best quality white bread and grate it and throw it into the boiling honey, and stir it all together with a spatula so that it doesn't burn to the pot. And then take it away [from the fire] and put in ginger, long pepper and edible sandalwood [for colouring it red], and mix it up with your hands; and then put it in a flat box [or make it into the shape of a flat box] and strew sugar on it, and place cloves around the edge and in the middle of it, if that pleases you.]

Ingredients:
225 g / 8 oz / 1 cup clear honey
6 cups / 1 white loaf of breadcrumbs (bread should be dried out or lightly toasted, but not stale)
2 tsps ginger
½ tsp black pepper

1 tbsp sugar
pinch of powdered cloves for flavour
red food colouring (to suit you)
a few whole cloves for decoration

Method: Bring honey to a boil, simmer two or three minutes, stir in breadcrumbs with a spatula until uniformly mixed. Remove from heat, stirring in ginger, pepper, a pinch of powdered cloves and any red food colouring (instead of the sandalwood used in the original). When it is cool enough to handle, knead it to get the spices thoroughly mixed. Either put the moulded mixture in a box or mould it into a flat box-like shape, sprinkle with sugar and put a few cloves ornamentally around the edge and in the middle if you want. Leave it to let the clove flavour sink in, but do not eat the cloves. An alternative way of doing it is to roll it up into small balls and then roll those in a mixture of sugar and ground cloves, and lay them on a dish or in a box decorated with cloves.

Notes: Long pepper (*Piper longum*, of the family *piperaceae*) is in the same family as black pepper (*Piper nigrum*), but is less hot. The whole spike of *Piper longum* berries is used, and is picked before the berries ripen, then dried. *Piper nigrum* is the source of both black and white pepper. To get black pepper, the unripe peppercorns are sun-dried, causing the outer skin to turn black and wrinkle. For white pepper, the ripe berries, having turned red, are soaked, then the outer covering is rubbed off. Long pepper is native to India, and is now very difficult to find in Britain, so I have substituted white pepper in this recipe.[18]

The gingerbread was a hugely popular dish at the Edible Exhibition, owing to its peppery flavour, and many guests went away with the recipe to try it out. Making the breadcrumbs can be quite time-consuming, but the flavour is well worth it.

Finally, I turned to the mysterious 'subtlety' which was a feature at the end of most of the courses given to royalty at fourteenth-century banquets. The name 'subtlety' referred to the fact that the food presented was made to look like something else, for example, eagles with real feathers made to look as if they were alive, or a saffron covered meatball mix with pastry 'prickles' made to resemble 'hirchones' or hedgehogs (urchins), in recipe 184 in *The Forme of Cury*. Even the 'four-and-twenty blackbirds baked in a pie' of the nursery rhyme was a 'subtlety' – the rhyme goes on to ask 'wasn't that a dainty dish to set before a king?'

The subtleties were sometimes made of pastry, and there is a description in *The Forme of Cury* of how to make pastry castles ('chastletes') with towers containing various fillings. The recipe included instructions to carve the castle crenellations carefully in the manner of battlements, and dry them hard in an oven or in the sun. One sort of stuffing for the castle turrets was made of pork and spices, another of almond cream, and another of cow's cream and eggs to be coloured red with edible sandalwood ('saundres'). Yet another turret was to be filled with figs, raisins, apples and pears, and the last mentioned is the filling for white fritters coloured green.[19]

Other subtleties were made of 'sugar plate', which was boiled sugar, and there is a recipe for this in *Goud Kokery*. The sugar plate described was a hard sugar substance rather than a fondant, because gum tragacanth (an agent to promote the making of more malleable fondant icing) had not yet been brought to Britain from the Middle East. This means that any modelling has to be done by pouring the sugar into moulds.

The fourteenth-century recipe given for sugar plate uses exactly the same principle as recipes for boiled sugar icing today, except for the modern additions of glucose (which breaks up the sugar crystals and makes the sugar more malleable), and cream of tartar (which prevents crystallization of the sugar and aids in the dispersal of the colouring agent).

In the royal court and in noble houses, where delicacies could be afforded, food was coloured with natural ingredients such as parsley or spinach to make a green colour, saffron for gold, 'saundres' (an edible variety of sandalwood) for red, and various lichens or tournesol to produce blue, pink or purple.

Tournesol (or turnsole) was extracted from the juice of a plant which grew in the sunny climate of France, Spain and Italy. After the juice was extracted, it was absorbed in cloths treated with alkaline substances, then dried and stored until needed. The reason the colour varied so much was that it was red when it was mixed with an acid substance, but turned blue or deep purple when it was put together with an alkali. There were many names for it in medieval times (for example *tournesol-en-drapeau* and *tournesol de Provence*), and its name was often linked to the technique of extraction and preservation in the cloth rather than the colour itself.[20] The deeper colours, which were used in manuscript inks as well as in food, were rare and very popular, and seemed to be traded over much of the known world.

Tournesol is suggested for the colouring of sugar plate (below), and the directions given include 'one ounce of fine tournesole, washed clean at the first boiling'. It would seem that the cloth was inserted into the sugar mixture at a certain point, allowing the dye to run out and colour the icing, and then removed when the cloth had been 'washed clean'.

The fourteenth-century recipe for sugar plate is a joy to read, and has quite useful and interesting directions. At one point we are instructed to stir the molten mixture 'evermore' with the spatula. It certainly seems like 'evermore' when you are waiting for the sugar to set! Another instruction caught my eye as well – we are asked to set the pan on the heat again for the amount of time it takes to say an 'Ave Maria'. In those days, everyone would have known how long that was, because this prayer would have been prayed many times a day in most households. For my own satisfaction, I recited the prayer aloud in Latin, to find that it takes about 30 seconds to chant it in the sonorous way it would have been delivered.

SUGER PLATE

To make SUGER PLATE. Take a lb. of fayr clarefyde suger and put it in a panne and sette it on a furneys, & gar it sethe. And asay þi suger betwene þi fyngers and þi thombe, and if it parte fro þi fynger and þi thombe þan it is inow sothen, if it be potte suger. And if it be fyner suger it will haue a litell lower decoccioun. And sete it þan fro the fyr on a stole, & þan stere it euermore with a spature till it

tourne owte of hys browne colour into a ȝelow colour, and þan sette
it on þe fyre ageyn þe mountynance of a Aue Maria, whill euermore
steryng wyth þe spatur, and sette it of ageyne, but lat it noght wax
ouer styfe for cause of powerynge. And loke þou haue redy beforne a
fair litel marbill stone and a litell flour of ryse in a bagge, shakyng
ouer þe marbill stone till it be ouerhilled, and þan powre þi suger
þeron as þin as it may renne, for þe þinner þe platen þe fairer it is. If
þou willt, put þerin any diuerse flours, þat is to say roses leues, violet
leues, gilofre leues, or any oþer flour leues, kut þem small and put þem
in whan þe suger comes firste fro þe fyre. And if þou wilt mak fyne
suger plate, put þerto att þe first sethyng ii unces of rose water, and
if ȝe will make rede plate, put þerto i unce of fyne tournesole clene
waschen at þe fyrst sethynge.[21]

[Translation: Take a pound of good clarified sugar and put
it in a pan and set it on a furnace and make it boil. And test
your sugar between your fingers and your thumb, and if it
comes off your finger and thumb then it is now cooked, if it is
ordinary sugar. And if it is finer sugar, it will have a little lower
decoction. And then set it away from the fire on a stand, and
then stir it continuously with a spatula until it turns from its
brown colour into a yellow colour, and then set it on the fire
again for the amount of time it takes to say an Ave Maria, while
continuously stirring with the spatula, and take it off again, but
do not let it get too stiff because it needs to be poured. And see
to it that you have a good little marble stone ready beforehand
and a little rice flour in a bag, shaking it over the marble stone
until it is covered, and then pour your sugar on it as thin as it
may run, for the thinner the plate the better it is. If you will,
put various kinds of flowers in there, that is to say rose petals,
violet petals, clove pink petals, or any other flower petals: cut
them small and put them in when the sugar first comes from the
fire. And if you wish to make fine sugar plate, put two ounces
of rosewater in it at the first boiling, and if you wish to make
red plate, put in one ounce of fine tournesole, washed clean at
the first boiling.]

Ingredients:
700 g / 1 ½ lbs white granulated sugar
300 ml / 10 ½ fl oz / 1 ½ cups water
125 ml / 4 ½ fl oz / ¾ cup liquid glucose
½ tsp cream of tartar

Method: You will need a large stainless steel pan to boil the sugar; heat-resistant gloves; a pastry brush and cup of water next to the stove; either a slightly oiled marble slab or a large sheet of parchment paper on a flat and level surface and a bowl of cold water large enough to set the cooking pot into when you take it off the heat.

Put the sugar into a medium-sized bowl and add cream of tartar. Mix the two ingredients together so the cream of tartar is dispersed properly and is not lumpy. Pour the water into a large (5 pint) stainless steel pot. Put the sugar and cream of tartar mix into the water. Add the liquid glucose.

Turn on heat to medium-high. Stir the pot constantly with a silicone spatula until all of the sugar crystals have dissolved, usually to the boiling point. Once at the boil, do not stir any longer, but wash down the sides of the pot with a pastry brush and water. It's important to keep any sugar and crystals off the sides of the pot. Put a sugar thermometer into the pot.

When the sugar reaches 140 °C / 280 °F you can add any food colouring you like, or the flowers that the recipe suggests. When the sugar reaches 160 °C / 317 °F remove the pan from the heat, and place it into the bowl of cold water to stop the cooking, then set it aside for one minute before pouring it onto the marble slab or parchment, being careful not to let it get too close to the edges. Cool and aerate the icing by first rolling it from the cooling edges, then folding it together, and letting it cool in stages while rolling, pulling and twisting it to aerate it, and finally flattening it and cutting up what you don't use into manageable pieces to store for later use.

Goud Kokery also gives instructions for making models out of sugar. Although the bakers in the fourteenth century would not have had access to gum tragacanth, they did have gum arabic. Gum arabic (the hardened sap of the acacia tree) is a binder, stabilizer and glue, and this was used to stabilize the sugar plate and also to glue the pieces of sugar plate together to form 'ymages' (the sugar mouldings described in recipe below).

YMAGES IN SUGER

To make YMAGES IN SUGER. And if ȝe will make any ymages or any oþer þing in suger þat is casten in moldys, sethe þem in þe same manere þat þe plate is, and poure it into þe moldes in þe same manere þat þe plate is pouryde, but loketh ȝoure mold be anoyntyd before wyth a litell oyle of almaundes. Whan þei are oute of þe moylde ȝe mow gylde þem or colour þem as ȝe will. Ȝif ȝe will gilde þem or siluer þem, noynte þem with gleyre of a egge and gilde þem or siluer þem, and if ȝe will make þem rede take a litell pouder of brasyll and boyle it a litell whyle wyth a litell gum araby, and þan anoynt it all abowte and make it rede. And ȝif ȝe will make it grene, take ynde wawdeas ii penyweȝte, ii penyweyte of saffron, þe water of þe gleyre of ii egges, and stampe all wele togeder and anoynte it wyth all. And if ȝe will make it lightly grene, put more saffron þerto. And in þis maner mow e caste alle manere froytes also, and colour it wyth þe same colour as diuerse as e will, and þer þat þe blossom of þat per or appell schull stand put þerto a clowe, & þer þe stalke schall stand makes þat of kanell.[22]

[Translation: If you want to make any images or anything out of sugar that is cast in moulds, boil it in the same way as the plate, and pour it into the moulds in the same way that the plate is poured, but see to it that your mould is coated beforehand with a little almond oil. When they are out of the mould, you may gild them or colour them as you wish. If you wish to gild them or make them silver, coat them with the white of an egg and gild them or make them silver, and if you wish to make them red, take a little brazil nut powder and boil it a short while with a little gum arabic, and then anoint it all around and make it red. And if you wish to make it green, take two pennyweight of indigo woad, two pennyweight of saffron, and the water of the white of two eggs, and beat it all together well and rub it on. And if you wish to make it light green, put more saffron in it. And in this way you can cast all manner of fruits also, and colour them with colours as diverse as you wish, and there where the blossom of pear or apple should be put a clove there, and the stalk should be, make that of cinnamon.]

Method: The fourteenth-century instructions for the sugar images are self-explanatory, and the use of metal moulds is similar today. We still coat the moulds with oil, and glaze our products with white of egg. Although we do not use most of the colouring agents mentioned, the principle of mixing the colours is the same, and we can get colouring pastes, gels or powders to achieve the same results. The hints on how to make the apple blossom out of a clove, and the stalk out of cinnamon are still good suggestions today.

Notes: I used either icing or marzipan to make subtleties for the Edible Exhibitions. Marzipan (first called 'marchpane' in Britain) is made with almonds, and these were widely available at the time. I made the subtleties with the more malleable form of the sugar plate (modern recipe above) so that I could mould the images instead of pouring the molten sugar into moulds, but do use moulds if you have them.

The 'subtleties' that were made in early centuries celebrated people and events that were special to the hosts and guests, so to celebrate fourteenth-century Oriel, I made a 'subtlety' in the shape of Oriel's first medieval buildings, which have long since been removed to make way for what is now the beautiful seventeenth-century First Quad. I modelled these buildings from sugar paste and marzipan, and mixed several teaspoons of cinnamon and ginger into the 'stone' of the building to give it flavour, and also to imitate the grain and colour of the Oxford ashlar stone, which sits, mellow and golden, in the sunlight of an Oxford evening. This ended the feast in the

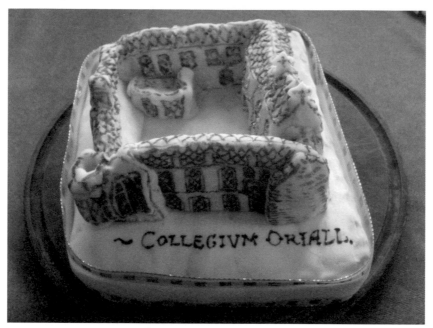

A 'subtlety' in the shape of Oriel College, prepared for the Edible Exhibition.

proper fourteenth-century fashion of the court by treating the guests to an edible sugar creation which unexpectedly resembled one of the buildings of the past.

The event made such an impression on one guest (Dr Peter Nockles, Rare Books Librarian at The John Rylands Library, Manchester), that he took the idea back with him and convinced the chefs at the University of Manchester to make dishes using translations from their own manuscript copy of *The Forme of Cury* – recipes are for sharing, after all!

Chapter Two

To the Manor Born

FIFTEENTH CENTURY

During the fifteenth century the world was alive to new ideas. The first European printing press was developed around 1440 by Johannes Gutenberg, and the first European printed world map appeared in 1472. America had been newly discovered, and many of the early printed books found in Oriel College from the fifteenth century contained early maps, picturing lands and civilizations far away from Britain. The maps and illustrations in these early travel books were not always accurate, but they give a picture of the world view of their time.

Oriel has a copy of a finely illustrated book entitled *Rudimentum novitiorum* ('A Handbook for Beginners') and this work was printed in Lübeck, Germany, in 1475. Many of its hand-coloured illustrations are of biblical scenes and people, and are there to teach readers about their heritage, while others show landscapes of European towns which all resemble the beautiful Lübeck. Included in the illustrations is a full page *mappa mundi* (an early map of the known world). The globe pictured is vividly coloured and divided into quarters, with the pillars of Hercules drawn at the foot of the map supporting the world, according to the Latin myth. The owner, who would have bought the book hot off the press, has inked in the word 'America' just outside the map's top left quadrant. He must have done this just after he had heard about America being discovered in 1492! The world was changing, and it was exciting.

Printing brought more knowledge to educated people of the time, and books started to appear in the vernacular language of the area, rather than in Latin or Greek only. The first printed cookbook (published in 1474) was that of Italian writer Bartolomeo Sacchi (1421-1481), who was also known as Platina, after his birthplace Piadena. His cookbook, *De honesta voluptate et valetudine* ('On Honourable Pleasure and Health'), was more of a treatise than the kind of recipe book we know today.

The first cookery book to be printed in English was entitled *This is the Boke of Cokery*, and it started with the words 'Here begynneth a noble boke of festes ryalle and cokery'. It was 'Emprynted without temple barre by Rycharde Pynson, in the yere of our lorde. M.D. [1500]'.[1] The book would have appealed to – and only been affordable for – the nobility and rich householders.

The earliest recipe book in English was not printed until 1500, so fourteenth-century English cooks and chefs would still have been working from written manuscript copies of their recipes for everyday use, if indeed they needed written recipes at all. One such manuscript is preserved in Corpus Christi College Library, just across the way from Oriel. I arranged with the archivist, Dr Julian Reid, to see Corpus Christi MS 291, which was entitled 'Divers receits' ('Various recipes').

After going through the beautiful high-ceilinged sixteenth-century library of Corpus Christi College, with its arched windows, medieval reading desks, and tall dark book presses, I was led downstairs to the cool, dry basement (the former wine-cellar) where the manuscripts and archives are now kept. There I was able to examine the dainty pocket-sized manuscript containing no less than ninety-nine recipes from the late fifteenth century.

According to the records, this little dark brown calf-bound volume had been given to Corpus Christi College Library between the dates of 1697 and 1714, as it is included in the description of books which could only have been presented to the college within that time span. It is described as an 'old book of receipts', and old it would have been when it was given to Corpus in the opening days of the eighteenth century. Most of the recipes are readable, and written in a tidy, flowing script, with no food stains and smudges like the ones that are on my own cookbooks. This book would have been much too precious to use with one hand on the cookbook and the other mixing the ingredients!

We do not know the history or provenance of the book before it arrived in Corpus, so we cannot establish when the various recipes were bound into the cover we see today. It is fairly tightly bound, so it is possible it was collected only as a record of the dishes used, and may not actually have resided in the kitchen at all.

What I most wanted to read in the manuscript were various recipes for sweet dishes that I had found in recipe books elsewhere, so that I could compare them, and write workable recipes for distribution. I took particular note of the recipes for 'Dareals' or 'Dariolles' (small custard tarts), 'Rastone' (stuffed loaves called 'rastons'), and 'Crustade' (fruit custard tarts).

It was wonderful to read the recipes straight from the fifteenth-century page, imagining the chefs and servants hurrying about in the kitchen; but I was given a further glimpse into life in a fifteenth-century manor when I found another book that had been bequeathed to Oriel Library: *The Household Book of Dame Alice de Bryene, of Acton Hall, Suffolk, Sept. 1412–Sept. 1413*, the manuscript of which was originally written in Latin and only published in English translation for the first time in 1931.

Alice de Bryene's husband, Sir Guy de Bryene, had died in 1386, leaving his young widow to form a household and run it with the aid of her stewards and other staff. Alice de Bryene kept careful accounts during this year, including what she spent on various items and services, the number of people who ate in her household per day, and some of the food they had to eat.

To read these accounts accurately, it must be understood that the English currency at the time (and up until 1971) was composed of pounds, shillings and pence. The shortened form (l.s.d.) which appears in the accounts below, comes from the Latin: *libra, solidus* and *denarius*. The pound sterling as we know it today was originally a pound in weight, and there were twenty shillings (*solidi*) in a pound and twelve pennies (*denarii*) in a shilling. In the fifteenth century, the pennies would have been further divided into two half pennies (pronounced ha'pennies) or four farthings (quarters of a penny).

Here is Alice de Bryene's account of her spending under the heading 'Wardrobe' for the year 1412-1413. The term 'wardrobe' seems to have come from the idea of the Royal Wardrobe, which was a storage facility not only for clothes, as we would expect, but for anything else that could be kept in storage for long periods of time without perishing:

For 20 lb. almonds bought at Steresbreg [i.e. Stourbridge] 4s 2d.; and for one frail [basket] of figs and one frail of raisins bought at Colchester, 6s. 10d. ; and for 7 lb figs bought at Stoke [Nayland] in the month of December, 7d. In 4 lb. raisins from Valencia bought there, 6d.; in 2 lb. raisins of Corinth [reysynz de corenz, i.e. currants] bought there, 7d.; in one lb. dates, 4d ; in one quarter of sugar bought there, 4 ½ d.; and for 4 lb. rice bought at Ster[esbreg] 3s. 3d. ; in 2 ½ lbs pepper bought at London, 8s. 6d. ; and for one quarter of sugar bought at Bur[y] in the month of February, 5d. ; and for one lb. saffron bought at Steresbregg 13s. ; and for 2 lb. ginger bought there, 3s. 4d. ; and for one lb. cinnamon bought there, 4s. 6d. ; and for one lb. soda-ash (sauudrez) bought there 12d. ; and for one lb. cloves bought there 3s. 4d. ; and for one lb. mace bought there 3s. 8d. ; and for one gallon 1 ½ quarts honey bought of Alexander White, 19d. ; and for one pottle honey bought from John White, 7d. Sum of the money, 56s. 10 ½ d.[2]

These accounts give us a very clear picture of the spices and dry goods Dame Alice bought during the year, and this informs our thinking about the ingredients her cooks would have used in their sweet recipes.

The goods were bought from various places in the region. Pepper was bought in London, which was about sixty miles away. Almonds, rice, saffron, ginger, cinnamon, cloves and mace were bought from 'Steresbreg'. This refers to the Stourbridge Fair, a famous annual late summer fair which was first set up at a cattle crossing near Cambridge at the start of the thirteenth century and continued for more than 700 years. Although it was about thirty miles away from Acton Hall, it would have provided the household with trade goods from other countries at the best prices possible, and the journey would have been worthwhile. For example, I discovered that some Oxford colleges regularly sent staff to buy fish and other provisions at Stourbridge Fair. The accounts of both Corpus Christi College and All Souls College record this.

Two 'frails' of raisins and figs were bought during the year from the town of Colchester, which was fifteen miles to the south of Acton Hall. A frail[3] was a large basket mainly designed to hold raisins and figs. It was made of woven rushes and held up to 75 lb of fruit.

More figs, raisins from Valencia, currants (whose name came from 'raisins of Corinth', which are dried Black Corinth grapes), dates, and sugar were bought from Nayland (now Stoke-by-Nayland) which is approximately nine miles to the south of Acton Hall, and six miles north of Colchester. Sugar was bought from Bury St Edmunds, which was about fourteen miles to the north.

Closer to home, over a gallon of honey was purchased from Alexander White, and a pottle (half a gallon) from John White, who were both neighbouring farmers.

Luxuries such as spices were expensive, and none more so than the golden saffron, which cost 13 shillings per lb; by contrast, almonds cost just over 4 shillings for 20 lbs. Saffron is extremely expensive even today, as there are still no automated methods of picking the individual stamens from each crocus. The amounts spent on spices and provisions are brought into focus when we see that the wage paid to workers in the household was typically only 3d. per day.[4]

Another ingredient in the list of purchases from Stourbridge Fair was printed as 'sauudrez' or 'sauudres', which was translated by Miss M.K. Dale in her edition of *The Household Book* as 'soda ash'. I wondered if this might be a washing or cleaning agent, but it was also mentioned later in the book under the heading of 'spices', so I tried to puzzle out what it would have been used for in this context.

Soda ash was the name given to sodium carbonate – an alkaline substance formed from certain kinds of soda-rich soil, kelp or seaweed. The main use of sodium carbonate was in the manufacture of glass, used by Egyptians from the earliest times, but the Romans also used it for medicinal purposes (to treat colic and skin eruptions), and as a raising agent in the making of bread. I thought that the latter was the most likely explanation, but try as I might, I couldn't find a recipe for medieval bread which included soda ash. It didn't cost much – only 12d. (or one shilling) per lb.

I then found a short notice in *The English Historical Review* for October

1932 which addressed the question directly. In a note about *The Household Book*, the reviewer said: 'The translation by Miss M.K. Dale is mainly satisfactory, and enough of the original is given in brackets to enable corrections to be made when needed as they sometimes are. Thus *sauudres* is more likely to be Alexanders than soda-ash...'[5] I am of the opinion that the 'sauudrez' or 'sauudres', mentioned is 'saundres' or 'sanders' (the red sandalwood colouring that was used constantly in the recipes of the age). I haven't yet been able to have a look at the original, but I would say that Miss Dale mistook the written 'n' in the accounts for a 'u'. It is also more likely that the term refers to 'sanders' than the suggested 'Alexanders', which, according to the herbals of the age, was the wild herb *Myrnium Olusatrum*, or in common usage 'wild parsley' or black lovage, which was to be found in any field, and would not have to be bought.

Alice de Bryene and her household would have eaten together every day in hall, a custom reaching back to earlier centuries, and still common today in colleges and large houses. There were guests at her table regularly, and it was not unusual for there to be as many as ten for breakfast, and over twenty for other meals throughout the day. From Christmas Day until the New Year 1412, a harper was present every day for all meals, and on New Year's Day, thirty were at breakfast, and more than a hundred at dinner.

There are no menus in the household book, but we can assume from the list of ingredients bought throughout the year that the company enjoyed desserts regularly. The household made their own bread and used a lot of it. Every several days, the bakers made about 240 white, and 30 black loaves from one quarter of wheat (a quarter of wheat weighed 28 lbs, i.e. a quarter of the old 'hundredweight' measure), and in the tally of food used for the meals of the day on Monday 17 October 1412, with six guests at each meal, the account reads: '50 white, and 7 black, loaves, of which newly baked 18 white, and 2 black, loaves'.

Presumably, the white loaves were pandemayn or wastel bread, the best bread, for which the flour had been twice-boulted (that is, passed through a fine straining cloth or sieve twice, to aerate it and to winnow out all the husks of wheat). I thought at first that the 'black' loaves would have been made of rye flour or maslin (a mixture of wheat and rye), but according to the records Alice de Bryene did not purchase any rye flour in this year and the loaves were all made from wheat, so the 'black' must refer to bread which had either not been boulted at all, or was not quite as finely sieved as the 'white'.

One of the earliest recipes we have for bread is the recipe in Bartolomeo Sacchi's *De honesta voluptate et valetudine*:

> *Therefore I recommend to anyone who is a baker that he use flour from wheat meal, well ground and then passed through a fine sieve to sift it; then put it in a bread pan with warm water, to which has been added salt, after the manner of the people of Ferrari in Italy. After adding the right amount of leaven, keep it in a damp place if you can and let it rise… The bread should be well baked in an oven, and not on the same day; bread from fresh flour is most nourishing of all, and should be baked slowly.*[6]

For the fifteenth century themed 'Edible Exhibition', I used recipes from contemporary cookery books for bread and 'rastons' (stuffed loaves) in order to reflect the high use of bread in the households of the time. These were to be found in both Corpus Christi MS 291, and the fifteenth century cookery books edited by the Early English Text Society. I chose the recipe from Harleian MS 279 (written around 1430), from *Two Fifteenth-Century Cookery-Books* as it specified a yeast-based bread to make the rastons, whereas the Corpus Christi recipe did not.

Brede and Rastons

Take fayre Flowre, & þe whyte of Eyroun, & þe ȝolke, a lytel; þan take Warme Berme, & putte al þes to-gederys, & bete hem to-gederys with þin hond tyl it be schort and þikke y-now, and caste Sugre y-now þer-to, & þenne lat reste a whyle; Þan kaste in a fayre place in þe oven, & late bake y-now; & þen with a knyf cutte yt round a-boue in maner of a crowne, & kepe þe cruste þat þou kyttyst; & þan pyke al þe cromys withynne to-gederys, an pike hem smal with þin knyf, & saue þe sydys & al þe cruste hole with-owte; & þan caste þer-in clarifiyd Boter, & Mille þe cromeȝ

& þe botere to-gedereȝ, & keuere it a-ȝen with þe cruste þat þou kyttest a-way; þan putte it in þe ovyn aȝen a lytil tyme; & þan take it out, & serue it forth.[7]

[Translation: Take good flour and white of egg and a small amount of yolk; then take warm yeast, and put all these together and beat them together with your hand until it is thick enough, and put enough sugar in it, and then let it rest a while; then put it in a good place in the oven and let it bake enough; and then cut the top of it around with a knife like a crown, and keep the crust that you have cut; and then pick all the crumbs inside together and pick them small with your knife, and save the sides and the outer crust whole, and then put clarified butter inside and mix the crumbs and the butter together, and cover it again with the crust that you had cut away, then put it in the oven again for a short time, and then take it out and serve it forth.]

Ingredients for the bread:
45 g / 3 oz 3 / tbsps dry yeast (or 1 oz fresh yeast) mixed with 100 ml / 4 fl oz / ½ cup warm water and ½ tsp of sugar
325 ml / 12 fl oz / 1 ½ cups ale at room temperature
2 tbsps sugar
1 tsp salt
1 egg, lightly beaten
1.4 kg / 3 lbs / 6 cups unbleached flour

Method: Dissolve ½ teaspoon of sugar with the yeast in warm water and set it aside in a warm place until it is frothy (usually about 15 minutes). Leave all the other ingredients out at room temperature – the rule for making bread is to keep all the ingredients warm, as opposed to pastry, where all the ingredients should be kept cold.

Combine ale, yeast mixture, sugar, salt and beaten egg in a large bowl. Add 4 cups of flour and blend ingredients by stirring with a large spoon. Turn dough onto a floured board and begin to knead it. As you knead, work in an additional 2 cups of flour by sprinkling it on the top

Stuffed bread (Rastons).

before folding the dough over and over again on itself. Stop adding flour when the dough loses its stickiness. Knead for about 10 minutes, or until smooth and elastic.

Put the dough into a bowl or basket. Cover with a moistened cloth and set it in a warm place for one hour or until doubled in size, then pummel the dough down with your fist 25 to 30 times. Divide it into 2 or 4 portions. Shape each portion into a round loaf, and place the loaves on a greased baking sheet. Score the top and make six or eight diagonal slashes around the perimeter to encourage the bread to rise while baking. If you want the top crusts to turn golden, brush them with milk. Bake in a preheated 190 °C / 375 °F / gas mark 5 oven for about 30 minutes. When it is done, the bread should sound hollow when you knock it on the bottom.

Notes: The word 'y-now' meaning 'enough' is repeated time and time again in many of these recipes, including the one for bread, above. This conveys the reality of traditional baking. The baker has so much experience that he or she can see and feel the progress of the baking every step of the way.

RASTONS

The rastons are like simple 'subtleties'. They are meant to surprise guests, because they look like ordinary loaves, but have an unexpected flavoured stuffing under the 'crown'.

Ingredients:*
1 round loaf of white bread
110 g / 4 oz / ½ cup slightly salted butter

* You could also add poppy seeds, or a teaspoon or so of cinnamon and a few raisins if you like, although the recipe does not specify this).

Method: With a sharp knife, cut the top crust off the bread in the zigzag shape of a crown. Lift off the crust and set it aside. Take out the soft bread and make it into crumbs, and melt the butter in a frying pan. Toss the crumbs in butter until they are evenly coated. Mix with poppy and/or fennel seeds. Replace the buttered crumbs in the loaf and put the top crust back into place. Reheat in moderate oven (180 °C / 350 °F / gas mark 4) for a few minutes before serving.

Notes: It was very satisfying to make the rastons with their 'crowns' to hide the stuffing inside. We included cinnamon and raisins as well as the buttered crumbs in some of the rastons that we made, in order to vary the menu.

Many of the Lenten recipes in medieval cookbooks call for almond milk or cream, rather than cows' milk, because on fast days, milk and eggs were left out (think of pancakes on Shrove Tuesday, which were made because people were encouraged to use up all their milk and eggs before they had to fast for Lent). I came across several recipes for cold almond milk, and although you can buy almond milk readily in shops these days, a thicker almond milk can be made using these recipes. I chose one from Harleian MS 279:

Fride Creme of Almaundys

Take almaundys, an stampe hem, an draw it vp wyth a fyne thykke mylke, y-temperyd wyth clene water; throw hem on, an sette hem in þe fyre, an let boyle onys: þan tak hem a-down, an caste salt þer-on, an let hem reste a forlongwey or to, an caste a lytyl sugre þer-to; an þan caste it on a fayre lynen clothe, fayre y-wasche an drye, an caste it al a-brode on þe clothe with a fayre ladel: an let þe clothe ben holdyn a-brode, an late all þe water vnder-nethe þe clothe be had a-way, an þanne gadere alle þe kreme in þe clothe, and let hongy on an pyn, and let þe water droppe owt to or .iij owrys; þan take it of þe pyn, an put it on a bolle of tre, and caste whyte sugre y-now þer-to, an a lytil salt; and ȝif it wexe þikke, take swete wyn an put þer-to þat it be noȝt sene: and whan it is I-dressid in the maner of mortrewys, take red anys in comfyte, or þe leuys of borage, an sette hem on þe dysshe, an serue forth.[8]

[Translation: Cold Almond Cream. Take almonds, and grind them, and strain them to a fine thick milk, mixed with clean water, set it on the fire and let it boil once, then take it off, put salt in it, and let it rest for 6-12 minutes, the time it takes to walk a furlong [200 metres] or two, and put a little sugar in it, and cast it on a good linen cloth, well washed and dried, and scatter it all about on the cloth with a good ladle: and let the cloth be stretched out, and let all the water underneath the cloth be taken away, and then gather all the cream in the cloth and let it hang on a pin, and let the water drip out for two or three hours; then take it off the pin, and put it in a wooden bowl, and scatter sufficient white sugar on it, and a little salt, and if it is too thick, put sweet wine in it that can't be seen [white wine?] and when it looks like a dish of pounded meat normally looks, take red anise, or borage leaves, and set them on the dish, and serve forth.]

Ingredients:

110 g / 4 oz / ½ cup blanched almonds (to blanch almonds, boil them
  in water for 2-3 minutes. Drain. Pour cold water over them and take
  off the skins)
ice water
125 ml / 4 fl oz / ½ cup boiling water
125 ml / 4 fl oz / ½ cup single cream (warmed)
some sweet white wine if needed
1 ½ tsps sugar
pinch of salt

Method: Grind blanched almonds in a blender or mortar, adding a
few tablespoons of ice water during the process to prevent the paste
from becoming oily. If you enjoy a crunchy texture, leave them coarse;
otherwise crush them completely to powder. Add sugar and salt to
½ cup of boiling water and ½ cup of warmed cream, and dissolve.
Pour liquid over almonds. Allow to soak about 10 minutes, stirring
occasionally. Strain out almonds if a smooth texture is desired, and
then add some warmed sweet white wine if the mixture is too thick.
Store in refrigerator and use as needed. The amount will last about 3
days and yields about 1 cup.

Notes: This description of straining the almond milk reminds me of
my mother making rose-petal or crab-apple jelly with the aid of her
finely meshed cotton and linen jelly bag. She would hang it up by its
string handles on a wooden peg above the kitchen windowsill and
leave it dripping for hours into a pan until all the liquid had been
strained out and she was left with a stiff jelly.

There are two parts of this recipe that particularly intrigue me. The first
one is the measurement of time needed to let the almond milk rest after
it has been boiled. Bearing in mind that none of the cooks would have
watches or other timepieces, they measured the time in familiar terms.
The time it would take for a man to walk a furlong (200 metres) would
be about 6 minutes, so that was their measure for this action. The other
intriguing part of the recipe is that they knew the almond milk mixture
looked right when it was 'I-dressid in the maner of mortrewys', that is,

like the pounded meat or fish that made up some of the common dishes they would have seen prepared for the table (for example, 'mortrewes of fysshe', 'mortreus de chare' or 'white mortrewys of pork').

The following recipe for pancakes is one which uses almond milk in Lent:

CRUSTE ROLLE

Take fayre smal Flowre of whete; nym Eyroun & breke þer-to, & coloure þe past with Safroun; rolle it on a borde also þinne as parchement, rounde a-bowte as an oblye; frye hem and serue forth; and þus may do in lente, but do away þe Eyroun, & nym mylke of Almaundys, & frye hem in Oyle, & þen serue forth.[9]

[Translation: Pancakes. Take good, fine wheat flour; break eggs into this, and colour the pastry with saffron; roll it on a board until it is as thin as parchment, and round as a communion wafer; fry it and serve it forth; and you may do this in Lent, but take away the eggs, and take almond milk, and fry it in oil and serve forth.]

Cruste rolle.

Ingredients:
¼ tsp pulverized dried saffron or 15 strands of saffron
2 tbsps boiling water
225 g / 8 oz / 1 cup plain white flour
pinch of salt
knob of butter or lard
2 eggs or 75 g / 3 oz / ⅓ cup of almond milk
lard or olive oil for frying

Method: Steep the saffron in the boiling water (or half water and half almond milk) until the liquid is deep gold in colour and has cooled. Sift the flour and salt and rub in the fat until the mixture is like fine crumbs. Beat the eggs (or almond milk) with the saffron water and use this to bind the flour, making a firm dough which is not too dry. Add extra cold water if needed. Roll out the dough as thinly as possible and cut it into 12-15 cm / 5-6 in rounds, using a small plate as a guide. Thinly grease a girdle or large heavy frying-pan with lard. Add the dough rounds, one at a time, and fry on a moderately hot surface, turning once, until browned on both sides.

Notes: It's interesting that we would still use the expression 'as thin as parchment' to describe how thin this kind of pastry ought to be, but the expression describes it well. The saffron gives these crusty rolls a lovely colour and the exotic saffron taste. The taste is further enhanced if you use one tablespoon of hot almond milk as well as a tablespoon of boiling water to soak the saffron, and also use almond milk instead of eggs. If the cooking of the pancakes can be done at the last minute, and close to where the event is taking place, the dish will be deliciously hot when served.

When I made the bread, I wondered what would have been eaten with it in the Middle Ages, and one possible accompanying food which came to mind was cheese. I had read that cheddar cheese was popular in the early centuries: a Somerset pipe roll – a collection of financial records kept by the English Exchequer – from 1170, during the reign of King Henry II, records the purchase of 10,240 lbs of cheddar cheese at a farthing per lb which meant a cost of £10 13s 4d – ten pounds, thirteen shillings and fourpence – a large amount of money in those days.[10] Knowing that cheddar was eaten during the fifteenth century, we served smoked cheddar cheese with the bread.

We also made quince and pear paste to serve with the bread. Quinces were a very popular choice of fruit in those days, and there were far more quince trees then than there are today. Fortunately, one of the members of Oriel had a quince tree growing in her garden, so we were able to try it out. It took quite a while to cook, and needed a fair bit of patience, but was worth it in the end. The recipe comes from Harleian MS 4016, written in about 1450 AD – the later of the two cookery manuscripts in *Two Fifteenth-Century Cookery-Books*.

CHARED CONEYS, OR CHARDWARDON

Take a quarter of clarefied hony, iij. vnces of pouder peper, and putte bothe to-gidre; then toke 30 coynes & x wardones, and pare hem, and drawe oute þe corkes at eyther ende, and seth hem in goode wort til þey be soft. Then bray hem in a morter; if they ben thik, putte a litull wyne to hem, and drawe hem thorgh a streynour; And þen put þe hony and þat to-gidre, then sette al on the fire, and lete seth awhile til hit wex thikke, but sterre it well with ij. sturrers, for sitting to; and þen take it downe, and put þere-to a quarter of an vnce of pouder ginger, And so moche of galingale, And so moche of pouder Canell, And lete it cole; then put hit in a box, And strawe pouder ginger and canell there-on: And hit is comfortable for a mannys body, And namely fore the Stomak. And if thou lust to make it white, leue the hony, And take so moch sugur, or take part of þe one and part of þe oþer/ Also in this forme thou may make chard wardon.[11]

[Translation: Quince or pear paste. Take a quart of clarified honey, 3 ounces of powdered pepper, and put both together; then take 30 quinces and 10 pears, and peel them, and take out the cores at each end, and simmer them in good unfermented beer until they are soft. Then grind them in a mortar; if they are too stiff, add a little wine to them, and strain them through a strainer, then put this with the honey mixture, then set it all on the fire, and let it boil a while until it becomes stiff, but stir it well with two stirring sticks; and then take it off the heat, and put in a quarter of an ounce of powdered ginger, and the same amount of galingale, and the same amount of cinnamon, and let it cool; then put it in a box and shake powdered ginger and cinnamon on it; and it is comfortable for a man's body, and especially for the stomach. And if you want to make it white, leave out the honey, and take the same amount of sugar, or take part of the one and part of the other/ Also in this way you can make pear paste.]

Ingredients:
1 kg / 2 ¼ lbs quinces or pears peeled, cored and cut into small wedges
225 ml / 8 fl oz / 1 cup of sweet red wine
500 g / 18 oz / 2 ¼ cups honey or sugar
2 tsps black pepper
½ tsp ginger
½ tsp galangal (or 1 tsp of ginger if you can't find galangal)
½ tsp cinnamon

Method: Cook quinces or pears in a pan with wine and black pepper until tender, cool off and either grind the mixture with a mortar and pestle, or put it in a blender until a fine purée is formed. Mix the honey or sugar with fruit purée and all the rest of the spices, and cook under constant heat, stirring with a wooden spoon until the mixture becomes sticky and comes off the sides of the pan.

Cover the bottom of a baking tray with parchment paper and spread out the mixture 6 mm / ¼ in thick, and smooth with a spatula. Let dry in a warm spot – at room temperature – for a couple of days, then cut into inch squares, or smaller if preferred, cover in sugar if you want, shake off the excess sugar and store in a tin, airtight, separated by parchment paper layers. The paste can also be left in a single large square and sliced off when needed.

Notes: When I first looked at this recipe, I thought it was for stewed rabbits (or 'coneys'), but what I assumed was 'coneys' proved to be the word 'coyns' (quinces) with the letters rearranged. Spelling was very fluid in those days, as it was not until 1604 that an English dictionary (or *A Table Alphabeticall*, as it was called) was attempted by Robert Cawdrey, a schoolmaster and former clergyman. I was very happy when I realized that the recipe was for a sort of quince paste or stiff jelly that would go beautifully with bread and cheese. The fact that the quinces and the spices used in this recipe were thought to be good for the stomach would have appealed to people of the age, as they were keen to bake food that was beneficial to health. I used a blender to mix the quinces, as they are quite hard to grind otherwise, and together with the spices, they made a very tasty accompaniment to the bread.

There are two recipes in several cookbooks of the time which have 'Lombardy' in their titles: 'Leche Lumbarde' (Lombardy slices) and 'Crustade Lombarde' (Lombardy custard). Cookery in the Lombardy region was well advanced, and the chefs made use of local fruits and spices.

The first recipe from Lombardy is a sliceable confection. There are at least three recipes for the sweetmeat called 'Leche Lumbarde' – one stiffened mainly with egg yolks, one with almonds and the one below (from Harleian MS 279), with dates:

Leche Lumbarde

Take Datys, an do a-way þe stonys, & sethe in swete Wyne; take hem vppe, an grynd hem in a mortere; draw vppe þorw a straynoure with a lytyl whyte Wyne & Sugre, And caste hem on a potte, & lete boyle tylle it be styff; þen take yt vppe, & ley it on a borde; þan take pouder of Gyngere & Canelle, & wryng it, & molde it to-gederys in þin hondys, & make it so styf þat it wolle be lechyd; & 3if it be no3t styf y-nowe, take hard 3olkys of Eyron & kreme þer-on, or ellys grated brede, & make it þicke y-now; þen take clareye, & caste þer-on in maner of a Syryppe, when þou shalt serue it forth.[12]

[Translation: Lombardy slices. Take dates, and take out the stones, and simmer in sweet wine; take them up and grind them in a mortar; sieve them with a little white wine and sugar, and put them in a pan, and let them boil until the mixture is stiff; then take it up and put it on a board, then take powdered ginger and cinnamon, and press it and mould it together with your hands and make it so stiff that it can be sliced, and if it is not stiff enough, crumble hard yolks of egg on it, or else grated bread, and make it stiff enough; then take aromatic wine, and pour it on like syrup, when you serve it.]

Ingredients:
12 stoneless dates
225 ml / 8 fl oz / 1 cup red wine and 1 tbsp white wine
8 tbsps white sugar
¼ tsp ginger
¼ tsp cinnamon
2 hard-boiled egg-yolks or 3 oz grated bread, if needed

Method: Simmer the dates in the red wine, then grind them with a mortar and pestle (or put them in a blender), sieve them with white wine and sugar, then bring them to the boil and let them simmer until they are stiff. Add the ginger and cinnamon, and if it is not stiff enough to mould, add sieved egg yolks or breadcrumbs to the mixture. Mould it into a brick shape and chill until cold and firm. Do not use the syrup if you are serving these as finger food, because it is too messy. Instead, cut them into small slices or cubes.

Notes: These little slices are packed full of flavour, rich and sweet. Keep them from being sticky by tossing them in a mixture of ginger and cinnamon to coat them.

The second recipe from Lombardy, 'Crustade Lombarde', was a favourite even in the fourteenth century – as we have seen, this dish was served in the first course of the coronation feast of King Henry IV in 1399. The name 'crustade' comes from the 'crust' which held the filling, but it has now come to mean the egg and cream filling itself.

CRUSTADE LOMBARDE

Take gode Creme, & leuys of Percely, & Eyroun, þe ȝolkys & þe whyte, & breke hem þer-to, and strayne þorwe a straynoure, tyl it be so styf þat it wol bere hym-self; þan take fayre Marwe and Datys y-cutte in .ij or .iij and Pruneȝ; & putte þe Datys an þe Pruneȝ & Marwe on a fayre cofynne, y-mad of fayre past, & put þe cofyn on þe ovyn tyl it be a lytel hard; þanne draw hem out of þe ouyn; Take þe lycour and putte þer-on, & fylle it vppe, & caste Sugre y-now on, & Salt; þan lat bake to-gederys tyl it be y-now; & ȝif it be in lente, lef þe Eyroun & þe Marwe out, & þanne serue it forth.[13]

[Translation: Lombardy custard. Take good cream, and parsley leaves, and yolks and whites of egg, and break them in the mixture, and strain them through a sieve, until it is so firm that

Crustade Lombarde
(Lombardy custard tarts).

it stands up by itself; then take good marrow and dates cut into two or three pieces, and prunes, and put the dates, prunes and marrow in a pastry case made of good pastry, and put the pastry case in the oven until it gets a little hard; then take it out of the oven. Take the liquid mixture and put it in, and fill it up, and put sugar and salt in it; then bake it all together until it has baked enough; and if it is Lent, leave out the eggs and marrow, and then serve it forth.]

Ingredients:
Shortcrust pastry (see pages 27-8 for ingredients and method)
10 each of prunes, stoneless dates and dried figs, cut into small pieces
3 tbsps finely minced parsley
225 ml / 8 fl oz / 1 cup double cream
2 tbsps brown sugar
2 eggs, lightly beaten
pinch of salt

Method: Prick the bottom and sides of the pastry case all over with a fork, fill it with baking beans or flour, and bake it at 220 ºC / 425 ºF / gas mark 7 for 10 minutes. Let it cool. Line the pastry case with dried fruits. Distribute the parsley evenly over the fruit. Combine remaining ingredients in a bowl, and beat until thoroughly blended. Pour over fruits in the pastry case. Bake at 190 ºC / 375 ºF / gas mark 5 for about 20 minutes or until custard is set and top is brown. Let the crustade cool before serving.

Notes: This resembles a fruit flan, and is quite a simple dessert to make. The only surprising element in it is the parsley, which adds a fresh flavour to it. The Corpus Christi MS 291 also has a recipe for 'Crustade', but it uses pears, apples, dates and raisins, and leaves out the prunes, figs and parsley – it also asks for pepper, saffron, edible sandalwood ('saundres'), cinnamon and 'lids' of pastry on top of the pie. Perhaps these differences are accounted for in the fact that the Corpus Christi recipe (No. 98) is not a recipe from Lombardy.

There are other small 'custard tarts' amongst the recipes of the fourteenth and fifteenth centuries named 'doucettes' and 'daryoles'. Daryoles were usually filled with eggs and cream, and sometimes herbs, fruits and spices, all mingled together. They resemble the baked custard tarts which you can still get at bakeries today.

I chose the recipe for 'Yellow Daryoles' from Corpus Christi MS 291 to illustrate these creamy melt-in-your-mouth pastries. This manuscript is unique in giving accurate quantities for the main ingredients – certainly a great help to us, the bakers of the future!

Dareals ʒelowe

Tak þe ʒelkes of eyryn; swynge hem, strayne hem into a bolle. Cast þerto creme, & menge þerwith. Cast þerto hony clarifyid & saffroun & salt. Mak cofyns & prik hem in þe botme; set hem in þe ovene. Fel hem with þes ʒelkes. Bake hem & ʒif forht.
A quart of creme, xl egges is ynow for xx cofyns.[14]

[Translation: Yellow custard tarts. Take the yolks of eggs, whisk them, strain them into a bowl. Put cream into this and make a mixture. Add clarified honey, saffron and salt to it. Make pastry cases and pierce them at the bottom; set them in the oven. Fill them with the yolk mixture. Bake them and give forth. A quart of cream, 40 eggs is enough for 20 pastry cases.]

Ingredients:
Shortcrust pastry (see pages 27-8 for ingredients and method)
6 egg yolks
450 ml / 16 fl oz / 2 cups double cream
50 g / 2 oz / ¼ cup clear runny honey
5-10 strands saffron, crushed
¼ tsp sea salt

Method: Soak the crushed saffron in 2 tablespoons of hot water until the water is deep gold in colour. Use the pastry to make small tarts if you prefer – this mixture makes 24 small tarts or 15 muffin-sized tarts with ¾ of each tart case filled.

Whisk the egg yolks lightly in a bowl, then beat in the cream, milk, honey, saffron water and salt. Pour the custard mixture into the pastry case. Bake at 160 ºC / 325 ºF / gas mark 3 for about 30-40 minutes or until each tart is firm, golden, and just set in the centre.

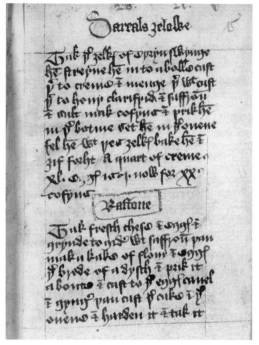

Corpus Christi MS 291, with the recipe for dareals.

Notes: If you are making small tarts, the pastry cases do not have to be baked in the oven beforehand; the pastry and the custard mixture will bake through at the same time. I have even tried making the tiny 'petit four' size of pastry cases to get double the amount, and this can be a good idea for trying out these unusual tastes to see if you like them, without having to eat too much until you have made up your mind. Allow to cool completely and refrigerate before serving. A delicious variation worth trying is almond cream instead of dairy cream.

The next dessert that we made for the event was 'Pynade', or pine nut brittle.

PYNADE

*Take Hony & gode pouder Gyngere, & Galyngale, & Canelle, Pouder
pepir, & graynys of parys, & boyle y-fere; þan take kernelys of Pynotys
& caste þer-to; & take chyconys y-sope, & hew hem in grece, & caste
þer-to, & lat seþe y-fere; & þen lat droppe þer-of on a knyf; & if it
cleuyth & wexyth hard, it ys y-now; & þen putte it on a chargere tyl
it be cold, & mace lechys, & serue with other metys; & ȝif þou wolt
make it in spycery, þen putte non chykonys þer-to.*[15]

[Translation: Pine-nut brittle. Take honey and good powdered
ginger, and galangal, and cinnamon, powdered pepper and grains
of paradise and boil them together; then take pine nut kernels and
put them in; and take boiled chickens and cut them up in fat,
and put them in, and let them simmer together; and then let it
drop from a knife; and if it sticks and becomes hard, it is cooked
enough; and then put it on a large serving dish until it is cool,
and make slices, and serve it with other meats; and if you want to
make it as a sweetmeat, then don't put any chickens in it.]

Ingredients:
450 g / 1 lb /2 cups honey
¼ tsp ginger
½ tsp galangal
¼ tsp cinnamon
¼ tsp black pepper
¼ tsp grains of paradise
1 cup pine nuts

Method: Put honey, spices, and pine nuts into a saucepan and bring
to a boil. Keep boiling the mixture until it reaches 150 °C / 300 °F
('hard crack stage'). Pour onto a baking sheet or piece of foil. Allow
to cool and then break it into small pieces and serve.

Notes: This is an exceptionally tasty, peppery nut brittle, which we chose to
make *without* the chicken. Grains of paradise are seeds with a cardamom-

like peppery taste from an African plant, and you can buy them in some shops and markets. If you can't find galangal in the shops, put in more ginger as a substitute – the roots of the two plants are very similar.

We wrapped the pieces of 'pynade' in brown paper, like treacle toffee is wrapped, because it can become a little sticky in the warmth of the room. If you make it, please warn your guests to hold the toffee in their mouths first to warm it and soften it up before biting into it, as it is quite hard, and might dislodge a tooth filling. I had thought that fillings for teeth were new phenomena, but it turns out I was wrong – our decaying teeth have been filled with substances such as beeswax or bitumen for thousands of years. One guest did ignore our warnings, and his teeth stuck together, but no more harm was done!

Gingerbread is an old favourite, and is usually made in a slightly different way every time. The recipe below does not mention ginger in the ingredients at all, but the powdered black pepper makes it gingery enough to suit the taste of most people.

GYNGERBREDE

Take a quart of hony, & sethe it, and skeme it clene; take Safroun, pouder Pepir, & þrow þer-on; take gratyd Brede, & make it so chargeaunt þat it wol be y-lechyd; þen take pouder Canelle, & straw þer-on y-now; þen make yt square, lyke as þou wolt leche yt; take when þou lechyst hyt, an caste Box leves a-bouyn, y-stykyd þer-on, on clowys. And ȝif þou wolt haue it Red, coloure it with Saunderys y-now.[16]

[Translation: Gingerbread. Take a quart of honey, and boil it, and skim it clean; throw in saffron and powdered pepper and take grated bread, and make it so stiff that it could be sliced; then take powdered cinnamon, and shake enough of it on; then make it square, ready to slice it; when you slice it, take Box leaves and arrange them on it, and stick cloves in it. And if you would like it red, colour it with the right amount of saunders.]

Ingredients:
450 g / 1 lb / 2 cups clear honey
pinch of powdered saffron
½ tsp ground black pepper
1 tsp of cinnamon
2 loaves (18 cups) fine white breadcrumbs or as needed
cinnamon and a few drops of red food colouring to coat as desired

Method: Bring the honey to the boil, reduce heat and allow to simmer for 5 to 10 minutes, skimming off any scum that forms on the surface. Take the pan off the heat and add saffron, pepper, cinnamon and bread crumbs (adding breadcrumbs a cup at a time). Mix well and scoop out into half inch sized portions. Put red food colouring in it if you like, form the mixture into small balls and roll them in cinnamon. Decorate with cloves and box leaves if desired.

Notes: The honey in the Middle Ages contained a lot more impurities than our processed honey does today, so you probably won't have to skim the honey you use if it comes from a shop rather than straight from the honeycomb. This gingerbread was a great favourite with everyone, and we ran out long before the end of the evening! If you are making it, be sure you make more than you think you'll need.

Quinces and pears were used a lot in baking in the fourteenth and fifteenth centuries, especially because they would be picked at harvest time, but would keep until January or February the following year. Warden pears were used in the recipes of these early centuries, and the variety was so popular that pears were referred to as 'wardons' or 'wardones'. The 'Old Warden' variety of pear has been recently replanted in England, because it had started to die out, and people wanted to be able to taste the pears that had become famous through medieval cookery. The following recipe could be used for either quinces or pears.

Quynces or Wardones in Paast

Take and make rounde coffyns of paast; and take raw quynces, and [pare] hem with a knyfe, and take oute clene the core; And take Sugur ynogh, and a litull pouder ginger and stoppe the hole full. And þen couche ij. or iij. quynces or wardons in a Coffyn and keuer hem, And lete hem bake; or elles take clarefied hony instede of sugur, if thou maist none sugur; and if þou takest [hony], put thereto a litull pouder peper, and ginger, and put hit in þe same maner in the quynces or wardons, and late hem bake ynogh.[17]

[Translation: Quinces or pears in pastry. Make round pastry cases, and take raw quinces, and pare them with a knife, and take the core out completely; and take sufficient sugar and a little powdered ginger to stuff the hole full. And then couch two or three quinces or pears in a pastry case and cover them, and let them bake; or else take clarified honey instead of sugar, if you don't have any sugar, and if you use honey, put a little powdered pepper into it, and ginger, and make it the same way for quinces or pears, and let them bake thoroughly.]

Ingredients:
Shortcrust pastry (see pages 27-8 for ingredients and method)
3-5 quinces or warden pears
¼ cup sugar mixed with 2 tsps ground ginger and a pinch of black pepper
¼ cup honey

Method: Make either a 23 cm / 9 in pie, or 12-18 tartlets instead of a large pie – the tartlets are better for a large event. If you are making a large pie, peel the quinces/pears, leave them whole and fill each one with honey/sugar and ginger, as it instructs in the recipe. Lay them in the pastry case, and put a pastry lid on top. If you are making individual tarts, quarter, core and slice the fruit and arrange the pieces tightly in the tart cases. Mix sugar, ginger and pepper, then add the honey, and spread over the fruit pieces. Cut pastry for the lids and cover. Bake at 180 ºC / 350 ºF / gas mark 4 for 60 minutes or until done.

Quince tarts.

Notes: It is possible that the pastry called for in this recipe was just a container for holding the fruit rather than for eating, as it does not specify that the pastry be 'faire', so the fruit in the large pie could have been designed to be taken out and eaten on its own as dessert at table. We made the pastry good enough to eat, and made small tarts, because they were more practical for an event where people were eating finger food.

Risschewes de Frute

Take ffigges, and grinde hem in a morter al smal with a litell oyle, and grynde with hem, clowes, and maces; and then take hem vppe in-to a dissh, and caste thereto pynes, saundres, reisons of coraunce, myced dates, pouder of Peper, Canell, Saffron, and salt; And then make fyne paast of floure, water, sugur, saffron, and salt, And make there-of faire kakes; and then rolle the stuff in thi honde, and couche hit in þe kakes; kutte hem, and so folde hem [togedrys] as risschewes, And fry hem in goode Oyle, And serue hem forthe hote.[18]

[Translation: Fruit rissoles. Take figs, and grind them finely in a mortar with a little oil, and grind along with them cloves and mace; and then put them into a dish and add pine nuts, sanders, currants, minced dates, pepper, cinnamon, saffron and salt; and then make fine pastry of flour, water, sugar, saffron and salt, and make this into fair cakes; and then roll the stuffing in your hand, and set it in the cakes; cut them, and fold them together as rissoles, and fry them in good oil, and serve them forth hot.]

Filling:
225 g / 8 oz / 1 cup figs
225 g / 8 oz / 1 cup dates
75 g / 3 oz / ⅓ cup pine nuts
50 g / 2 oz / ¼ cup currants
½ tsp cloves
½ tsp mace
¼ tsp black pepper
½ tsp cinnamon
¼ tsp salt
drop or two of red food colouring
pinch of ground saffron

Dough:
275 g / 10 oz / 1 ¼ cups flour
75 ml/ 3 fl oz / ⅓ cup water
3 tbsps sugar
½ tsp salt
pinch of ground saffron

Method: Grind figs and dates. Mix in pine nuts, currants and spices and set aside. Mix flour, sugar, salt and saffron. Add water a little at a time until it forms a soft dough. Cut dough into small pieces –

about an inch in diameter, and roll out as thinly as possible. Place a small amount of filling into the centre, fold the dough over, and press the edges to seal. Deep fry them in oil and serve them hot. (Makes about twelve.)

Notes: The same person who made the hot pancakes also made these tasty rissoles on site, and brought them to the event at intervals; hot, comforting and much appreciated in the cold December weather.

The subtleties in the fifteenth century were even more intricate than in the previous century. In a menu for the installation of John Stafford as Archbishop of Canterbury in 1443 AD, given in *Two Fifteenth-Century Cookery-Books*, three intricate subtleties are listed by which

the company honoured the new Archbishop.

The simplest subtlety, at the end of the first course, is described as: 'Seint Andrew, sitting on an hie Auter of a-state, with bemes of golde; afore him kneling, þe Bisshoppe in pontificalibus; his Croser kneling behind him, coped.'[19] ('St Andrew sitting on a high altar of state, with beams of gold; the bishop [John Stafford himself] kneeling before him in his bishop's vestments, with his crozier kneeling behind him, coped.') We are not told how this subtlety was made, or if it was edible. It may have been just for show, and certainly the assembly would have admired it as a work of art.

I chose to make an edible icing and marzipan image of some of the early Oriel College buildings as they would have appeared in the fifteenth century, and the guests enjoyed admiring it and eating it.

The Edible Exhibition to celebrate the fifteenth century was another success, and everyone went home the richer for a taste of the past, and for the conversation and friendship this experience encouraged.

CHAPTER THREE

DESSERT AT HIGH TABLE

SIXTEENTH CENTURY

Good hospitality has always been seen as an indicator of power, status, and hierarchy – as well as kindness – and dinner at High Table in an Oxford college in this Tudor age of pageantry and splendour was no exception. The High Table, as its name suggests, was raised on a shallow wooden platform or 'dais' above the rest of the company at their 'low' tables.

The whole college community would gather in the hall for dinner, much as they do today. The junior members in their gowns would assemble at the lower 'common' tables first, and the Fellows and guests would then file into the hall in order of seniority; a bell would be rung, and grace would be said in Latin by a Fellow or senior scholar to start the meal.

A typical place setting for each person would have included a trencher made of wood for most of the diners, a cup of wood, pewter or silver, a linen napkin, a small manchet loaf, and a pewter or silver spoon. In 1596, Oriel owned a 'dozen spoons one whole guilded the rest guilded on the endes have the pictures of the twelve apostles'.[1] The diner carried his own knife with him in a sheath.

Only the Head of House or special guests were given silver tableware, which was often engraved with the rank of the person who was permitted to use it. Although much of Oriel's silver was given over to the Royalist cause to be melted down during the English Civil War, there still remain later examples of the practice in Oriel: for instance, one moulded rat-tail tablespoon made in 1690-91 was inscribed '*In usum Communar in Aula*'[2] ('for the use of the Bursar in Hall'), and in a later example, six teaspoons with a fiddle and shell pattern were inscribed 'ORIEL COLLEGE | *IN USUM* | *PRAEPOSITI* | 1907'[3] ('Oriel College | for the use | of the Provost'). During the sixteenth century knives and forks were used at table for serving food rather than for eating, and diners would wash their hands afterwards in a ewer and basin supplied at table, or at a nearby sink.[4]

Trenchers (from the French *trancher*, 'to cut') had originated as thickly-cut slices of bread used as plates, the purpose of which was to soak up the juices of the meal and to be eaten afterwards. The diner would help himself to the food, taking care not to spill anything, and would lay the food on the trencher. He would put his salt on a small trencher to the side, as it was bad manners to put your knife back into the communal salt dish once it had been used in your own trencher. Wooden trenchers gradually replaced these, mainly to protect the tables from being scored with knife cuts, and the tablecloths soiled with spillages, but it is worth noting, as my husband reminded me, that an 'open-face' sandwich such as Americans enjoy could be thought of as a modern day trencher! There are examples of simple wooden trenchers with small circular hollows for salt still in existence at the Abingdon-on-Thames museum, amongst other places.

By the end of the sixteenth century, circular discs known as 'roundels' became a feature at special occasions rather than plain trenchers. Roundels were usually crafted of beech or sycamore wood which was cut very thinly, but they could also be made of other materials such as glass, silver, or pewter. The roundels were often decorated on one side with painted verses, drawings or paintings, and sometimes even musical notation.

Guests ate from the plain side of the roundel, then cleaned them with bread, and turned them over to reveal the decoration. If the roundels had poems or songs on them, these were read or sung by guests. The decorated roundel fitted into the Tudor fashion for entertainment during dining. This was still the age of magnificent subtleties and trompe l'oeil amusements, and the roundels themselves could even be made of sugar paste or marzipan like a subtlety, and eaten afterwards.

The manchet bread used at dinner was of the finest quality. The diner would pick up his bread in his left hand, place it on his trencher, slice it into strips and reassemble the whole thing back into place. If there was pottage or meat with gravy served, the bread would be dipped into the common dish with the left hand, and the rest would be eaten with a spoon. The left hand was for communal use – leaving the right hand for personal use – the knife was taken in this hand. The napkin was put over the left shoulder so that the diner could clean his lips on it without removing it. Bones were put in a small dish called a voiding dish.[5]

At the conclusion of the main course the 'Grace-cup' (typically a large and highly ornamented silver drinking cup) was sent up to the High Table, and after the final grace had been said, the Fellows filed out of the hall with their guests to go for their dessert.

The term 'dessert' first came into use at this period, and the word derives from the French *desservir*, meaning 'to remove what has been served', or in other words, to clear the tables. At court, college, and in many noble Elizabethan houses, the banqueting tables in the hall were filled to capacity with serving dishes from the main courses, and the servants had to be given time to clear the tables, so the final course was set out and served in another location – this could be in another room or even in a garden or summer-house.[6]

The tradition of going to a separate place for dessert is still followed today at High Table in Oxford colleges. Whenever the Head of House finishes the main course at the end of evening dinner, the guests still rise for grace (whether they have finished their main courses or not!), take their napkins with them as instructed, and go to another room where fruit and sweetmeats are set out, and various wines are passed around the table.

Recipes were traditionally handed down through families or from master to apprentice by word of mouth, and England's first printed cookbook, *This is the Boke of Cokery*, was published by Richard Pynson in 1500. Commonly known as the *Book of Cookery*, it was made up of many previous recipe manuscripts and menus of royal banquets. There is just one surviving copy of the book in the library of the Marquess of Bath at Longleat in Wiltshire.

Longleat is the family seat of the Thynnes, whose ancestor, William

Thynne, was a royal courtier. In 1524, William Thynne was second clerk of the kitchen in the household of Henry VIII, and by 1526 he had become chief clerk of the kitchen, with full control of royal banquets. By 1543 he was one of the two masters of the household for the king, and in the year of his death he appears to have been the sole master. In 1544 he had also become one of the officers of the counting house.[7] William Thynne also had an interest in printing, and brought out an edition of the works of Geoffrey Chaucer in 1532.

One type of book that was very popular in the sixteenth century was the 'herbal', and these large tomes had a great deal of influence on culinary habits. At this time, the study of plants was based on critical observation, and botanists (or herbalists as they were known) began to explore the use of plants for both medicinal and agricultural uses. Many of the writers became experts in identifying and describing plants, and the herbals they compiled included beautiful drawings, notes and paintings of plants that they had first sketched, then collected, and finally dried as specimens. The history of herbalism is closely tied with the history of medicine, and many of the herbs and spices approved as having medicinal properties were also used to season food, precisely because of their medicinal qualities.[8]

Herbals were organised by the names of the plants, their identifying features and therapeutic properties – and some (such as the herbal written by John Gerard in 1597), included instructions on how to prepare and use the plants. Recipe writers wanted to make sure they were using ingredients in their food which would benefit those eating it, so they relied on the herbals to give them advice. For example, John Gerard gives these notes regarding saffron: 'The chiues steeped in water, serue to illumine or (as we say) limne pictures and imagerie, as also to colour sundry meats and confections. The confections called *Crocomagna*, *Oxycroceum*, and *Diacurcuma*, with diuers other emplaisters and electuaries cannot be made without this Saffron.'[9]

Explorers such as Walter Ralegh and Thomas Harriot (both alumni of Oriel College), took herbals with them on their trips to South America and Roanoke Island to help them identify species and combat disease during their travels. Oriel College Library has many fifteenth-century herbals which were bequeathed to the college in 1600 by John Jackman,

a physician who had studied at Oriel, and one of these herbals was shown at this sixteenth century Edible Exhibition.

During the sixteenth century, the English language became more standardised. William Caxton, who was an English merchant, writer and printer, had introduced a printing press into England in 1476, and was the first English retailer of printed books. Caxton helped to standardize the English language through printing, by regularising regional dialects in favour of the London dialect. As a translator and printer of books, Caxton had to ensure that the language which he used was acceptable to the widest possible group of potential readers and buyers.

In the preface to the *Eneydos* (a translation of Virgil's *Aeneid*), Caxton discusses the problem of understanding varied dialects from the different counties of England. First he explains that there were many varieties of English, and that the English in one county differed from that spoken in another, then he illustrated this by telling a story of some merchants going down the Thames in a ship and landing in Kent to buy food. One of the merchants asked a woman if he could buy some 'eggys', but the woman thought he was speaking French, and she could not understand him, because in her dialect the word for eggs was 'eyren'. She said she didn't have eggys, and it was only when another merchant asked for 'eyren' that the woman finally understood, and said that she did have them.

Caxton then wrote: 'Loo what sholde a man in thyse dayes now wryte egges or eyren? Certaynly it is harde to playse euery man by cause of dyuersite and chaunge of langage.' ('Now, what should one write nowadays, eggs or eyren? It is certainly hard to please everybody because of the diversity and the change of our language.)[10]

Caxton's solution to this problem of the varieties of English was to try to use 'moderate and readable terms' and to do this he aimed his language at 'a clerke and a noble gentylman'. This compromise by Caxton was a very canny one, because he formed his text to reflect the speech of learned and (usually) rich gentlemen of influence who would buy his books and recommend them to others. This version of English was the language used by the scribes in Chancery, later called Chancery Standard English.[11]

The translation of the Bible and many other foreign works into

English, and the printing of well-known vernacular literature by writers such as Mallory and Shakespeare, helped to establish the market for English printed books of all types, and to raise the status of English not only within England itself, but also throughout the known world.

This standardization of the language meant that the recipes that were printed in the sixteenth century were more generally understandable than those in the manuscript copies which had gone before. As was the common practice, many of the cookbooks used recipes taken from other earlier recipe books and manuscripts, and were written by men, but for the first time they were aimed at a more general audience, including housewives who ran their households and needed practical advice on medicines, brewing, dairy work and preserving.

I did not find any contemporary culinary cookbooks in Oxford colleges, but did take a recipe from a modern facsimile of *A Proper Newe Booke of Cokerye*, which was first published around 1545.

Another recipe is from from *The Good Huswifes Jewell* (1585), by Thomas Dawson, and one from the 1591 edition of *A Book of Cookrye: Very Necessary for All Such as Delight Therin*, by an author signing as A.W., but most are from *The Good Huswifes Handmaide for the Kitchin*, also by Thomas Dawson, published in 1594. Here to start with is his recipe for fine manchet bread:

FINE MANCHET

Take halfe a bushell of fine flower twise boulted, and a gallon of faire luke warm water, almost a handful of white salt, and almost a pinte of yest, then temper all these together, without any more liquor, as hard as ye can handle it: then let it lie halfe an hower, then take it up, and make your Manchetts, and let them stand almost an hower in the oven. Memorandum, that of every bushel of meale may be made five and twentie caste of bread, and everie loafe to way a pounde beyside the chesill.[12]

[Translation: Take 20 lbs of flour which has been sieved twice through a fine cloth, and a gallon of lukewarm spring water, almost a handful of white sea salt, and almost a pint of ale yeast, then mix them together without any more liquid, as stiff as you can manage: then set it aside for half an hour, then take it and make your manchets, and let them bake almost an hour in the oven. Remember that from every bushel of meal you can make twenty-five castes of bread, and every loaf should weigh a pound in addition to the wholemeal bran ('chesill').]

Ingredients:
12 g / ½ oz dry yeast
150 ml / ¼ pint warm water
150 ml / ¼ pint warm ale
450 g / 1 lb plain flour
2 tsps salt
50 g / 2 oz softened butter

Method: Dissolve yeast in a mixture of warm water and ale. I use half ale to water in order to give it an authentic taste, but you can use just water if you like.

Put the flour into a large bowl with the salt. Make a well in the centre of the flour, pour in the yeast mixture and mix in the butter very well. Knead for 10-12 minutes, adding more flour if the dough is too wet. Cover the bowl with a cloth and put it into a warm place to rise for 1½ to 2 hours, or until it has doubled in size.

Knead the dough again for 4-5 minutes, and make into four small flat oval loaves and put them on two greased baking trays. Cover with a cloth and leave to rise for 40-45 minutes. If you wish the top crusts to turn golden, brush them with milk or beaten egg, and slash them across the top twice or three times.

Bake in a preheated oven at 190 °C / 375 °F / gas mark 5 for 35-40 minutes.

Notes: This bread was the best white bread that was available at the time, made with the finest flour it was possible to have. It was designed to be an accompaniment to the main course, but at the Edible Exhibition it was enjoyed as an hors d'oeuvre with quince jelly and cheese.

❦

The next recipe chosen was from a 1557 edition of *A Proper Newe Booke of Cokerye*, a copy of which is in the Parker Library of Corpus Christi College, Cambridge. It was thought to have been used by Margaret, the wife of Matthew Parker, the fourteenth Head or Master of the College.

Matthew Parker was a priest in Holy Orders, which was usual for the Heads of Oxford and Cambridge colleges until the last quarter of the twentieth century. It had been against the law for priests to marry, but he had married Margaret in 1547, after the laws governing the marriage of priests were repealed by Edward VI. However, when Queen Mary came to the throne in 1553, she enforced the annulment of the Edwardian act of permission for priests to marry, thus forcing married clergymen to 'put away' their wives.

The Parkers had lived happily in the Master's Lodge at Corpus Christi until then, but Matthew Parker did not want to separate from his wife, so he felt that he had to resign the Mastership and take his family to live in the country. On Mary's death, Elizabeth was released from the Tower of London and made Queen of England. She subsequently asked Matthew Parker, who had been chaplain to her mother, Anne Boleyn, to be Archbishop of Canterbury, and he agreed to do this in December 1559, whereupon the family moved into Lambeth Palace.[13] The Parkers had a great reputation for hospitality, and Margaret probably used the cookbook at this period. This recipe for a 'Tarte of Borage flowers' makes an attractive and refreshing dessert. Gerard says this about borage in his herbal: 'Those of our time do vse the floures in sallads, to exhilerate and make the mind glad.'[14]

TO MAKE A TARTE OF BORAGE FLOURES

Take borage floures and perboyle them tender, then strayne them wyth the yolckes of three or foure egges, and swete curdes; or els take three or foure apples, and perboyle withal and strayne them with swete butter and a little mace and so bake it.[15]

[Translation: Take borage flowers and parboil them until they are tender, then strain them with the yolks of three or four eggs, and sweet curds; or else take three or four apples, and parboil those and strain them with unsalted butter and a little mace and so bake it.]

Ingredients:
Shortcrust pastry (see pages 27-8 for ingredients and method)
1 tbsp fresh or dried borage flowers (cut up small)
110 g / 4 oz cream cheese or small curd cottage cheese
2 egg yolks, beaten
1 tsp mace
25 g / 1 oz caster sugar
100 ml / 4 fl oz double cream
25 g / 1 oz plain flour

Method: Set your oven at 200 ºC / 400 ºF /gas mark 6. To make the filling, simmer a small pan of water and sprinkle in the cut borage petals. Wet the petals thoroughly, then drain immediately through a fine sieve and lay to one side. Beat the sugar with the cheese until smooth,

Borage tart decorated
with crystallized borage flowers

then beat in the egg yolks, one at a time, followed by the cream. Stir in the mace, borage flowers and flour. Pour into a 20 cm / 8 in pastry case or individual tartlet cases and cook in the centre of the oven for about 30 to 35 minutes, or until firm to the touch in the centre. Decorate with crystallized borage flowers if possible (instructions below).

Ingredients for crystallized flowers:
1 large pasteurized egg white (or egg white substitute) and ½ tsp of water, or a mixture of 50 ml / 2 fl oz rosewater (or water) and 1 tbsp gum arabic
fresh flowers
50 g / 2 oz white superfine caster sugar

Method: At the outset, make sure the borage plant has not been sprayed with insecticides. If you have trouble with greenfly on your plant, shake up a solution of water and two drops of washing-up liquid in a small spray bottle, and spray the plant with that, and the plants will remain completely edible.

Take one pasteurised egg white, or egg white substitute, add the tablespoon of water, then fork it through gently to break up the albumen, but do not beat it.

If you wish to avoid using egg, you can mix gum arabic with rosewater as a glaze instead. To do this, stir the water/rosewater and gum arabic together in a jar. Probably the rosewater was originally used more for perfume than for practical purposes, so you can use a mixture of half rosewater and half tapwater if you like. When the gum arabic has dissolved into the water, it will form a honey coloured suspension. You can leave it in the jar for a few days if you wish.

Before you pick the flowers, get something ready to put them on to dry. You could use a wire rack, but I have found that the best method is to stretch some non-stick baking parchment over the top of a small rectangular container, and make holes in the top for each stem to sit in, with lots of space between each flower, so that the crystallized flowers can air dry for up to twenty-four hours.

Clip each flower from the plant, leaving a short amount of stem with the flower. This will be useful for drying, and for anchoring the flower

To dry them off properly the stem of each crystallized borage flower is put through a hole made in baking parchment spread over a tupperware container.

in the tart as decoration afterwards. Wash the flowers in cold water, and dry them thoroughly on paper towels. Take one fresh flower at a time by its stalk and remove the prominent black stamens with scissors, as some people may be allergic to them.

Use a very fine small paint brush to paint the egg/gum solution onto the front and back of every part of the flower. Dust back and front with caster sugar and leave them to dry for at least twelve hours, delicately poking them through the holes in the baking parchment.

Coat the flowers using a fine brush then follow the instructions above. They will last for a few months in a sealed airtight tin.

Notes: The recipe itself does not mention a pastry case, but as it is called a tart, I made a pastry case for it. You can make individual cases if you would prefer. Adding crystallized borage flowers makes a pretty decoration, and gives people an idea of what the flowers look like.

The next recipe is a typical Elizabethan tart of apples and orange peel, redolent of spices, with a delicate fragrance of rosewater to conjure up a summer day!

TARTES OF APPLES AND ORANGE PILLES

For a tarte of apples and orenge pilles. Take your orenges and lay them in water a day and a night, then seeth them in faire water and honey and let seeth till they be soft; then let them soak in the sirrop a*

83

day and a night: then take forth and cut them small and then make your tarte and season your apples with suger, synamon and ginger and put in a piece of butter and lay a course* of apples and between the same course of apples a course of orenges, and so, course by course, and season your orenges as you seasoned your apples with somewhat more sugar; then lay on the lid and put it in the oven and when it is almost baked, take Rosewater and sugar and boyle them together till it be somewhat thick, then take out the Tart and take a feather and spread the rosewater and sugar on the lid and let it not burn.[16]

* There is no need for a full translation of this recipe – it is fairly understandable by modern standards, and only two terms in it need an explanation. The term 'orenge pilles' means 'orange peel', and the term 'course' in this context means 'layer'.

Ingredients:
Shortcrust pastry (see pages 27-8 for ingredients and method)
5 medium oranges (i.e. bitter Seville oranges)
225 g / 8 oz / 1 cup honey
4 cups of the water which was used to soak the oranges
4 medium cooking apples, peeled, cored, and sliced 6 mm / ¼ inch thick
1 tbsp butter (melted)
110 g / 4 oz / ½ cup brown sugar
1 tsp cinnamon
½ tsp ginger
¼ tsp salt
1 tsp rosewater and 1 tbsp sugar for brushing the lid of the tart

Method: Soak the oranges in water for 24 hours. In a large saucepan, mix the honey with 4 cups of the water used to soak the oranges, add the oranges, bring to a boil, and simmer until the peels on the oranges feel soft. Put the oranges in a large bowl or other container and pour on all the syrup, then weigh them down with a lid or plate to hold them under the syrup. If there is not enough syrup to completely cover the oranges, add a little more water and let the oranges soak for another 24 hours. Meanwhile, make up your pastry, prick the bottom and sides of the pastry case all over with a fork, fill it with baking beans or flour, and bake it at 220 ºC / 425 ºF / gas mark 7 for 10 minutes. When the oranges are ready, slice them thinly and remove any seeds. Cut them into small pieces and mix with ⅓ cup of sugar, ½ teaspoon of cinnamon, and ¼ teaspoon of ginger.

Peel, core, and cut up your apples into slices 6 mm / ¼ in thick, and mix them with the remaining sugar, cinnamon, and ginger. Pour the melted butter on the pastry case, then put a layer of apples on the bottom of the case, followed by a layer of oranges on top of the apples. Repeat the layering until you have no more fruit (usually two layers of each fruit). Put on the pastry lid with any decorations you would like, crimp the edges together, and bake for an hour at 180 ºC / 350 ºF / gas mark 4. Just before the tart is ready, make up your rosewater and sugar mixture for brushing on the top lid, and stir it until it thickens into syrup, and five minutes before the tart has finished baking, take it out of the oven, brush the rosewater syrup over it and put it back into the oven to finish baking.

Alternative method: If you lack time, and would rather use commercial candied orange peel instead of using the longer method of soaking and cutting up the oranges, you can take ¼ cup freshly squeezed orange juice and ¼ cup candied citrus peel. Bring the orange juice, ⅓ cup of sugar, ½ teaspoon of cinnamon, and ¼ teaspoon of ginger to a boil. Simmer for 3-5 minutes, or until slightly thickened, and follow the recipe from the second paragraph, where the apples are cut up.

Notes: This is a very time-consuming recipe to make if you follow the instructions for soaking the oranges rather than using commercial orange peel, but in those early centuries, oranges would have appeared quite exotic and strange, and would have been a treat to prepare and eat. The lid of the tart was brushed with sugar and rosewater with a feather, and this is just right for the delicate crust of the pie. My Irish granny lived on a farm where chicken and duck feathers were plentiful, so she used feathers when baking all the time. Chicken wing feathers were best for brushing the flour across the bread board when she was making soda scones, and duck feathers were used to stroke the lids of the tarts with egg yolks if she wanted to brown them. The feathers would be discarded after use.

The following recipe for 'Pescoddes' is for a type of sweet pasty, a snack in the shape of a pea pod, and easily transported for eating while travelling or working. Some types of Cornish pasty are still made as a complete meal – half of the filling is savoury, and half sweet. These can be made as large or small as you like, and they are very tasty and enjoyable, and a talking point for guests.

PESCODDES

To make pescods another. Make your past with fine flower, and yolks of Egs, make it shorte and drive it thinne. Take Apples, and mince them small, take Figs, Dates, Corrans, great Raisons, Sinamon, Ginger, and Sugar, mince them, and put them all together, and make them in litle flat peeces, and frie them in Butter and Oyle.[17]

[Translation: Pea pods. Another way of making pea pods. Make your pastry with fine flour, and yolks of eggs, make it short, and roll it thinly. Take apples, and chop them up into very small pieces, take figs, dates, currants, raisins, cinnamon, ginger, and sugar, mince them all up together, and make them into little flat pieces and fry them in butter and oil.]

Shortcrust pastry (see pages 27-8 for ingredients and method)
1 apple chopped small
50 g / 2 oz / ¼ cup each of finely chopped figs, dates, currants and raisins
½ tsp ground cinnamon
½ tsp ground ginger
50 g / 2 oz / ¼ cup sugar
cinnamon and ginger for sprinkling
2 tbsps oil / butter for frying

Method: Mix up pastry. Mix fruits and spices together and then mix in the sugar. Roll pastry very thinly, and cut into 5 cm / 2 in circles. Spread

Pescoddes

a thin layer of fruit mixture across half of each round, fold it in half, and seal the edges so that it resembles a pea pod. Brown them in oil or butter. Sprinkle with cinnamon and ginger and serve.

Notes: Be careful to seal the edges of each 'pea pod' carefully. When spreading the fruit mixture, you can even place it in small mounds on the pastry so that the 'pod' looks as though it contains individual peas.

Almonds were still very popular to use in all sweet dishes, and this almond tart, with its additional rosewater, was a common addition to great feasts.

A TARTE OF ALMONDS

Blanche Almonds and beat them, and straine them &c, with good thicke Creame, then put in Sugar and Rosewater, and boyle it thicke: then make your paste with Butter, fair water, and the yolks of two or three Egs, and as soon as you have driven your paste, cast on a litle Sugar, and Rosewater, and harden your paste afore in the Oven. Then take it out, and fill it, and set it in againe, and let it bake till it be well, and so serve it.[18]

Ingredients:
Shortcrust pastry (see pages 27-8 for ingredients and method)
2 eggs (beaten)
110 g / 4 oz / ½ cup sugar
325 g / 12 oz / 1½ cups ground almonds
¼ tsp of salt
½ tsp almond essence

Method: If you are baking a large tart, bake the pastry case in the oven first at 220 ºC / 425 ºF / gas mark 7 for 10 minutes. Let cool, and mix all ingredients for filling together. Fill ¾ full with filling. Put in a 180 ºC / 350 ºF / gas mark 4 oven for about 20 minutes or until brown on top.

If you wish to make small tarts in individual cases, there is no need to bake the pastry in the oven beforehand, just fill each small case ¾ full, and pop them into the oven for about 15 minutes or until brown on top.

Notes: This is a rewarding and easy recipe to make, and can be made gluten-free if you would like. Rice flour or almond flour was available in these early centuries, and could be chosen as a flour for the basis of the pastry instead of wheat flour. These flours will make up a more crumbly pastry, because they lack gluten, so you may have to add a lightly whisked egg white or a little more water to the mix (start with one more tablespoon if it is too crumbly).

The next tart recipe is a fascinating one. The name 'A tarte to provoke courage either in Man or Woman' seems to refer to sexual courage, as many of its ingredients were deemed to be aphrodisiac. 'Burre' (burdock) roots, 'potaton' (potato – that is, sweet potato) roots, quinces, dates and even brains of cock sparrows were all in this category (although I have omitted this last ingredient in my recipe, substituting sweet chestnuts).

The white potato with which we are most familiar (*Solanum tuberosum*) was brought from the Americas to Britain by way of Ireland in the 1580s (probably by Walter Ralegh), but European and British people were already familiar with the sweet potato (*Ipomoea batatas*), which is the type included in the following recipe. Columbus had brought sweet potatoes back to Spain at the end of the fifteenth century, and Europeans referred to the sweet potato as the potato, which often leads to confusion. It wasn't until after the 1740s that the term 'sweet potato' began to be used by American colonists to distinguish it from the white (Irish) potato, and the white potato took many more years to reach the recipe books.

John Gerard wrote about the [sweet] potato in his *Herball* of 1597. Along with a description of the plant, he also describes how it is eaten (roasted and infused with wine, boiled with prunes, or roasted with oil, vinegar, and salt). He suggests that the sweet potato 'comforts, strengthens, and nourishes the body', and 'serves as a ground or foundation whereon the cunning confectioner or sugar-baker may worke, and frame many comfortable conserves and restorative sweetmeats…', as well as 'procuring bodily lust'.[19] This aphrodisiac quality could be the reason for the popularity of the 'courage tart' in sixteenth century England. Much was made of double entendres involving aphrodisiacs in Shakespeare's *The Merry of Wives of Windsor*, where Falstaff exclaims in this comic scene: 'Let the sky rain potatoes; let it thunder to the tune of 'Green Sleeves'; hail kissing-comfits and snow eringoes; let there come a tempest of provocation…' (Act V Scene v.)

A Tarte to Provoke Courage Either in Man or Woman

Take a quart of good wine, and boyle therein two Burre roots scraped cleane, two good Quinces, and a Potaton root well pared and an ounce of Dates, and when all these are boyled verie tender, let them be drawne throgh a strainer wine and al, and then put in the yolkes of eight Egs, and the braines of three or foure cocke Sparrowes, and straine them into the other, and a litle Rosewater, and seeth them all with Sugar, Synamon and Ginger, and cloves and Mace, and put in a litle Sweet Butter, and set it upon a chafingdish of coales betweene two platters, and so let it boyle till it be something big.[20]

[Translation: Take a quart of good wine, and boil in it two burdock roots scraped clean, two good quinces, and a sweet potato root well pared and an ounce of dates, and when all these are boiled until they are very soft, put them through a strainer, wine and all, and then put in the yolks of eight eggs, and the brains of three or four cock sparrows, and strain them into the other ingredients with a little rosewater, and boil them all up with sugar, cinnamon and ginger, and cloves and mace, and put in a little sweet butter, and set it on a chafing dish* of coals between two large plates, and so let it boil until it increases in size.]

* A chafing dish was a portable grate raised on a tripod, originally heated with charcoal in a brazier, and used for foods that needed gentle cooking, away from the flames. The chafing dish could be used at table or provided with a cover for keeping food warm. In this case it was protected 'between two platters'. A modern equivalent is the bain-marie used for lunches in most institutions today. This is a metal basin which floats in a hot water bath, used for keeping food at the right temperature to be served.

Ingredients:
Shortcrust pastry (see pages 27-8 for ingredients and method)
2 large sweet potatoes, peeled and diced, *or* 1 large sweet potato and 1 burdock root
450 ml / 16 fl oz / 2 cups sweet white dessert wine
2 soft crushed sweet chestnut kernels (boil chestnuts first for 35 minutes, then peel)
2 quinces or apples, peeled, cored and diced
6 chopped stoneless dates
2 tbsps light brown sugar
½ tsp each of ground cinnamon and ground ginger
a pinch each of ground cloves and ground mace
2 tbsps butter, softened

4 large egg yolks
1 tsp rosewater

Method: Put the sweet potatoes (and the burdock root if you can get one), wine, and pre-boiled sweet chestnuts in a small saucepan over medium-low heat and simmer for 10 minutes. Add the quinces/apples and dates, and simmer for 25 minutes, or until the quinces/apples are tender. (If the mixture becomes too dry, add one or two more tablespoons of wine.) Mix until smooth.

Preheat the oven to 180 ºC / 350 ºF / gas mark 4. Roll out the pastry on a floured board. Line a pie dish with the dough and trim off any excess.

Place the sweet potato mixture in a large bowl. Add the brown sugar, spices and butter, and stir until well combined. Beat the egg yolks and rose water in a small bowl, add to the filling, and mix well. Pour the filling into the pastry case and bake for 1 hour, or until the centre springs back when lightly pressed.

Notes: Most people at the Edible Exhibition were interested in this recipe, and there were many questions about the reason for the inclusion of the ingredients.

Savoury pies and tarts were still common in the sixteenth century, as they were easily divided and eaten by hand. Many of the larger pies and tarts were made in raised cases of a stiff pastry, and as there was a contemporary recipe for these raised 'coffins', it is included here. Tudors were very fond of making intricate patterns on their pastry, and there are plenty of pastry cutters available to create whatever shapes you wish to put onto your pie lid using any leftover pastry.

Tarte of Cheese

Make your tart, and then take Banberie Cheese, and pare away the outside of it, and cut the cleane cheese in small peeces and put them into the Tart, and when your Tart is full of Cheese: then put two handfuls of sugar into your Tart upon your cheese, and caste in it five or sixe spoonfuls of Rosewater, and close it up with a cover, and with a feather lay sweet molten Butter upon it, and fine sugar, and bake it in a soft Oven.[21]

TO MAKE PASTE AND TO RAISE COFFINS

Take fine flour and lay it on a boord and take a certaine of yolkes of Egges as your quantitie of flower is, then take a certain of Butter and water and boile them together but ye must take heed ye put not too many yolkes of egges, for if you doe it will make it drie and not pleasant in eating, and ye must take heed ye put not in too much Butter, for if you doe, it will make it so fine and so short that you cannot raise: and this paste is good to raise all maner of coffins: likewise if ye bake Uenison, bake it in the paste above named.[22]

Ingredients for a 20 cm / 8 in raised pastry case with lid:
550 g / 20 oz / 2 ½ cups flour
110 g / 4 oz / ½ cup butter
6 tbsps water
3 egg yolks

Method: Mix flour and egg yolks. Put butter and water in a small saucepan over low heat until the butter is melted. Add the butter and water to the flour and egg mixture. Knead until all the flour is absorbed into the dough. Divide the dough in half and roll out. It will not need to be chilled, as the texture of the pastry is stiff and solid, in order to make the sides stand up when they are raised to 2.5 cm / 1 in, or even 5 cm / 2 in high. Put the raised pastry case in a tin lined with baking parchment, ready to fill with the cheese mixture, and decorate the lid with cut pastry shapes if desired.

Filling:
3 egg yolks, lightly beaten
225 g / 8 oz / 1 cup Cheshire or similar cheese
275 ml / ½ pint / 1 ½ cups full-cream milk
2 tsps sugar

1 tbsp rosewater
25 g / 1 oz butter

Method: After you have made the raised pastry case, grate the cheese finely and soak it in the milk for at least 3 hours. Then blend them together, and rub them through a sieve. Mix in the sugar, egg yolks, rosewater and warmed but unmelted butter. Pour the mixture into the prepared tart case, put on the lid and bake at 180 ºC / 350 ºF / gas mark 4 for 40 minutes or until set and brown on top. Serve cold.

Original shortbread (the following recipe) was a type of 'bread biscuit' or twice baked biscuit made with dough left over after bread making, which was sweetened and made into biscuits. The word 'biscuit' comes from Italian and literally means 'twice cooked'. This 'shortbread' is a bit harder than we are used to, and we wouldn't consider it very special at all, but to people of the time, it would have been a luxury. Gradually, the leavening was replaced by butter, and the large amount of fat in the mixture gave the shortbread a more crumbly 'short' texture. Caraway seed was often added to the mix, and the dough would then be formed into fingers, rounds or the popular petticoat tails (a large circle divided into segments).

SHORT CAKES (SHORTBREAD)

Take wheate flower, of the fayrest ye can get, and put it in an earthen pot, and stop it close, and set it in an Oven and bake it, and when it is baken, it will be full of clods, and therefore ye must searse it through a search [sift it through a sieve]: the flower will have as long baking as a pastie of Venison [i.e. 35 minutes]. When you have done this, take clowted Creame, or els sweet Butter, but Creme is better, then take Sugar, Cloves, Mace and Saffron, and the yolke of an Egge for one doozen of Cakes one yolke is ynough: then put all these foresaid things together into the cream, + temper them al together, then put them to your flower and so make your Cakes, your Paste wil be very short, therefore yee must make your Cakes very litle: when yee bake your cakes, yee must bake them upon papers, after the drawing of a batch of bread.[23]

Ingredients:
110 g / 4 oz slightly salted butter straight from fridge, *or* 175 ml /
  6 fl oz double cream
1 yolk of egg (beaten)
50 g / 2 oz caster sugar
150 g / 5 oz plain flour
50 g / 2 oz rice flour
½ tsp saffron (optional)
a pinch each of cloves and mace

Method: In this recipe the flour is baked once by itself, and then baked again with the other ingredients so that it is crisp.

Heat your oven to 170 ºC / 325 ºF / gas mark 3, and put 150 grams

*Short cakes,
cut with a leaf cookie cutter,
and decorated with sugar paste.*

of plain flour in a small lidded pottery casserole dish lined with baking parchment for 35 minutes. Cool the flour off and then sift it into a bowl.

Mix together the sugar, cloves, mace, and saffron powder in a bowl. Stir in the beaten egg and then fold the mixture into the cream, or if you are using butter, work the grated butter quickly into the flour by rubbing it with your fingers, then stop when the mixture resembles breadcrumbs. Continue until you have a firm dough.

Turn the dough out onto a floured surface and knead gently, then roll it out and cut it into very small shapes (a leaf cookie cutter does this very nicely) and arrange on your lined baking tray, spacing them at intervals, as the mixture will spread a bit. Bake in the oven at 170 ºC / 325 ºF / gas mark 3 for 30-35 minutes until they are golden in colour. Prick them with a fork and leave them to cool on the tray.

Before this time in England, the sugar paste used for decoration and for making 'subtleties' had been made with gum arabic, so it had to be poured into moulds and hardened to keep its shape; but by the sixteenth century, gum tragacanth, a gum extracted from trees in the Middle East and first known in England as 'gum dragon' or 'gumma dragantis' had come to Britain through Italy. Gum tragacanth is soluble in water and binds with the sugar to form a malleable paste, making it easier to make into fondant.[24]

Thomas Dawson's recipe for sugar paste using gum tragacanth is from the 1597 edition of *The Good Huswifes Jewell*. The author describes it as 'A past of Suger, whereof a man may make al manner of fruits, and other fine things with their forme, as Plates, Dishes, Cuppes and such like thinges, wherewith you may furnish a Table.'

PAST OF SUGER

Take Gumme and dragant as much as you wil, and steep it in Rosewater til it be mollified, and for foure ounces of suger take of it the bigness of a beane, the iuyce of Lemon, a walnut shel ful, and a little of the white of an eg. But you must first take the gumme, and beat it so much with a pestell in a brasen morter, till it become like water, then put to it the iuyce with the white of an egge, incorporating al these wel together, this done take four ounces of fine white suger wel beaten to powder, and cast it into the morter by a litle and a litle, until they be turned into the form of paste, then take it out of the said morter, and bray it upon the powder of suger, as it were meale or flower, untill it be like soft paste, to the end you may turn it, and fashion it which way you wil. When you have brought your paste to this fourme spread it abroad upon great or smal leaves as you shall thinke it good and so shal you form or make what things you wil, as is aforesaid, with such fine knackes as may serve a Table taking heede there stand no hotte thing nigh it. At the ende of the Banket they may eat all, and breake the Platters, Dishes, Glasses, Cuppes, and all other things, for this paste is very delicate and saverous. If you will make a Tarte of Almondes stamped with suger and Rosewater of this sorte that Marchpaines be made of, this shal you laye between two pastes of such vessels or fruits or some other things as you thinke good.[25]

[Translation: Sugar Paste. Take as much gum tragacanth as you think will be appropriate, and steep it in rosewater until it is softened, and take four ounces of sugar (a bean-sized amount), a walnut-shell full of lemon juice, and a little of the white of an egg. But you must first take the gum, and beat it so much with a pestle in a brass mortar, that it becomes as runny as water, then put the lemon juice into it, with the white of an egg, incorporating all these well together, then take four ounces of fine white sugar well beaten to powder (i.e. icing sugar), and put it into the mortar little by little, until it is turned into a paste, then take it out of the mortar, and crush it to a powder along with the sugar, as finely as if it were meal or flour, until it is like soft paste, so that you can mould it however you like. When you have brought your paste to this form, roll it out into large or small 'leaves' – whatever is the right shape and size for making what you need, as I have said, using such clever tricks as you can to put on the table, but taking heed that nothing hot comes near it. At the end of the banquet they may eat all, and break the Platters, Dishes, Glasses, Cups, and all the other things you have made, for this paste is very delicate and appetizing.

If you will, make an Almond tart with beaten sugar and rosewater of the kind that Marchpanes are made of, and you can lay this between two paste 'plates' or make other such vessels or fruits or other things that you think would be good.]

Ingredients:
1 lightly beaten egg white (use pasteurized egg white if possible)
300 g / 11 oz sifted icing sugar
2 tsps gum tragacanth
1 tsp lemon juice
1 tsp rosewater
1 tsp water

Method: Soak the gum tragacanth in the rosewater and water until it softens. The tragacanth mixture should be slightly runny, not stiff or lumpy. If it is too stiff, add a bit more water. If you wish to colour your sugar paste with a liquid colouring such as saffron water, use it as the soaking liquid for the gum tragacanth instead of the plain water, rather than adding the colouring at a later stage.

Rub a cut lemon or some lemon juice around the inside of a large mixing bowl, and put the slightly beaten egg white into the bowl. Gradually add enough icing sugar to make the mixture come together into a ball.

Fold in the gum tragacanth mixture and lemon juice, and then put the paste on a board or work surface dusted with icing sugar, and knead it well until it is smooth and malleable. Mix in the rest of the icing sugar to achieve a stiff paste. Makes 350 g / 12 oz sugar paste.

Notes: You can use the paste to shape whatever you want. Keep the unused portions and any scraps in a plastic bag or cling film. Do not allow air to get to the paste, or it will harden.

If you add water-based food colouring rather than paste colour, do this with the liquids at the start of the recipe, before the icing sugar is added. You may need to add less liquid in the recipe and perhaps increase the amount of gum tragacanth to keep it flexible.

If you only want to colour part of the paste, break off the desired amount and knead in paste colours rather than liquid colours. You could also add spices such as cinnamon and ginger to the icing, to give it a great flavour and to give it the appearance of stone, if you are making the model of a building.

Use the sugar paste like modelling clay, and attach any sections that you need to put together with beaten egg white or icing made with egg white. Be careful not to add liquids after the paste has been mixed, as this will spoil it. Let your paste models dry for at least twenty-four hours.

Always keep your pieces of paste away from heat or moisture, and do not put them in the oven to dry. Do not put them in the fridge at any stage either, where they will dissolve into damp lumps. Believe me, it's a shock when this happens!

If you are putting the sugar paste in moulds, use a light coating of vegetable oil, or a dusting of icing sugar or cornflour to help the sugar paste come out of the mould.

This recipe for 'White gingerbread', made with a mixture of sugar paste and marzipan, is taken from *A Book of Cookrye: Very Necessary for All Such as Delight Therin*:

WHITE GINGERBREAD

Take Gumma Dragagantis half an once, and steep it in rosewater two daies, then put thereto a pound of sugar beaten & finely serced, and beate them well together, so that it may be wrought like paste, then role it into two Cakes, then take a few Jordain almonds & blaunch them in colde water, then dry them with a faire Cloth, and stampe them in a morter very finelye, adding therto a little rosewater, beat finely also the whitest Sugar you can get and searce it. Then take Ginger, pare it and beat it very small and serce it, then put in sugar to the almonds & beat them togither very well, then take it out and work it at your pleasure, then lay it even upon one of your cakes, and cover it with an other and when you put it in the molde, strewe fine ginger both above and beneath, if you have not great store of Sugar, then take Rice and beat it small and serce it, and put it in the Morter and beat them altogither.[26]

[Translation: White gingerbread. Take half an ounce of gum tragacanth, and steep it for two days in rosewater, then add to it a pound of sugar beaten and well sifted, and beat them well together, so that it can be handled like paste, then roll it into two separate 'cakes', take a few Jordan almonds and blanche them in cold water, then dry them with a good clean cloth, and crush them well in a mortar, adding a little rosewater, and beat well also the whitest sugar you can get and sift it. Then take ginger, pare it and crush it very small and strain it through a sieve, then put the almonds in the sugar and beat them together very well, then take [the mixture] out and work it at your pleasure, then lay it evenly upon one of your 'cakes', and cover it with the other and when you put it in the mould, scatter fine ginger both above and beneath. If you do not have a great store of sugar, then take rice and beat it well and sieve it, and put it in the mortar and beat them altogether.]

White gingerbread.

Ingredients:
225 g / 8 oz marchpane (almond paste)
15 g / 1 tbsp ground ginger
225 g / 8 oz sugar plate (fondant icing)

Method: Knead the ginger into the marchpane and roll it out on a board dusted with icing sugar to a thickness of about 6 mm / ¼ in.

Divide the sugar plate into two, and roll out one piece into the same size as the marchpane. Dampen one side of the marchpane, and place it damp side down on the sugar plate. Next, roll out the other piece of sugar plate, dampen the other side of the marchpane, place the sugar plate on top, and smooth it down. Then roll the marchpane and sugar plate (white gingerbread) sandwich to a thickness of around 6 mm / ¼ in.

Cut the gingerbread into small diamonds or rounds, or press the sections into moulds, trimming off the surplus with a knife, and leave to dry. Any unused trimmings may be kneaded together and cut into shapes as well.[27]

Notes: I used Peter Brears' method of making the white gingerbread, and it was absolutely delicious. I cut the 'gingerbread' into very small rounds, and stamped each of them with the centre of a Tudor Rose stamp that my brother had given me, and then rubbed in edible powder food colouring, to make it glow with all the tints of the rainbow!

The 'subtlety' that I made for this Edible Exhibition represented the Oriel buildings in the sixteenth century, as drawn by the draughtsman John Bereblock (1557–1572). The drawings complement Thomas Neale's inventive Latin text in a book that was made to be presented to Elizabeth I on her visit to Oxford in late August 1566. This manuscript is now in the Bodleian Library, and the Edible Exhibition cake was modelled on the copy of the manuscript which features in Louise Durning's edition of the

English translation, *Queen Elizabeth's Book of Oxford*.[28]

When I made the 'subtlety' of the manuscript, I kneaded cinnamon and ginger into the fondant icing to make it flavoursome, but also to lend it the appearance of an old manuscript. Drawings on the sugar paste may be done freehand or by transferring a pattern. To make the drawing and the script, I used a pen filled with edible brown ink – you can find these coloured pens now in many craft shops. To ensure I had a straight line on which to write the script, I made a copy of it from the book on tracing paper, put the paper over the icing 'page' and made pinpricks on the 'page' to mark out the lines, just as the scribes used to do to mark the end of their straight lines on the parchment when they were writing the original manuscript with inks. I used this method to 'trace' the outline of

A 'subtlety' baked in the form of a manuscript held in the Bodleian Library.

the drawing as well, and 'joined the dots' afterwards. It is time-consuming, but works well.

To set the scene, we played Tudor music in the background, and guests were invited to wear rich colours and fabrics so that they could form a living tapestry of Elizabethan life.

CHAPTER FOUR

THE LADY'S KITCHEN

SEVENTEENTH CENTURY

Recipes have been important from the beginning of civilization, and many of the recipes passed down through families and recorded in earlier ages were medicinal. When I asked librarians of other colleges if they had any manuscript recipe books in their archives or libraries, many said that the only ones they had were a few medicinal 'receipts'. The word 'receipt' from which we take our modern word 'recipe' (meaning a set of instructions for preparing a particular medicine or culinary dish), was first used in medieval English as a prescription for a medicinal preparation. Both forms of the word derive from the imperative of the Latin verb *recipere*, meaning 'to take back', therefore 'to take' or 'receive'. The imperative form was *recipe!* – 'take!' or 'receive!' (Giving and receiving – isn't that a great way of saying that recipes mean 'hospitality'?)[1]

According to the *Oxford English Dictionary*, the first word in the list of ingredients for a prescription was traditionally *Recipe*! This was often abbreviated to a letter R with a small bar through it, commonly called Rx, a symbol that still sometimes appears on modern prescription forms, especially in North America. The term 'recipe' has been used along with 'receipt' since the eighteenth century to refer to cooking instructions, and has now all but replaced it. Our modern meaning of 'receipt' meaning 'a written statement stating that money or goods have been received' comes from the beginning of the seventeenth century.

Recipe books written in the seventeenth century were often presented as documents whose secrets were known only to the few. The titles of these works (for example, *The Closet of the Eminently Learned Sir Kenelm Digby Kt. Opened* or *The Ladies Cabinet Enlarged and Opened*) speak of the secret nature of these books. The secrets in them were claimed to have been previously known only by kings and queens and knights of the realm.

The art of distillation was one of the secret arts which was important for a woman to learn. Distillation was linked to alchemy, which intrigued everyone during this time. Alchemy was the medieval forerunner of experimental chemistry, concerned with the transmutation of matter, in particular with attempts to transform base metals into gold or to find a universal elixir for all the ills besetting mankind.

During the Renaissance, 'science' and 'literature' were defined 'through a shared aesthetic that understood all knowledge production as an art – the art of 'making',[2] so making recipes was seen in much the same light as making poetry or writing about philosophy, or participating in alchemy.

Many domestic manuals were written for the use of women in the early part of the century. One of these, written by Sir Hugh Plat near the end of his life in 1602, was entitled *Delightes for Ladies to Adorn their Persons, Tables, Closets, and Distillatories: with Beauties, Banquets, Perfumes and Waters*. Another well-known domestic manual entitled *The English Huswife* was written in 1615 by Gervase Markham, the son of a courtier, after he had lived and worked for some years as a small landowner and husbandman.

These manuals, like others published at the time, were written in response to changing ideas of women's domestic duties, and described appropriate female conduct, education, and behaviour, as well as giving many medicinal and culinary recipes of the age.

As the century progressed, women themselves started to write and publish manuals and recipe books. Composing medicinal and culinary recipes was seen as an appropriate extension of household responsibilities, and so it was an acceptable form of writing for women when other avenues were closed.[3]

The seventeenth century was also the age of metaphysical poetry, with its 'conceits' and philosophical arguments, and this was reflected in the kitchen. One witty variety of sweetmeat illustrates the close correspondence between poems and recipes in the early seventeenth century. *A Closet for Ladies and Gentlewomen,* often assumed to have been written by Sir Hugh Plat, includes a recipe for 'walnuts' made of sugar paste, enclosing sweetmeats or poetry instead of nut-meats.

'WALNUT' SURPRISES

To make a Walnut, that when you Cracke it, You shall find Biskets, and Carrawayes or Fruits In It, Or a Prettie Posey Written. Take a piece of your Past Royall White, or Almond Past, being mixed with a little fine searced* cinnamon, which will bring your past into a Walnut shell colour, then drive it thinne, and cut it into two pieces, and put the one piece into the one half of your mould, and the other into the other, and put what you please into the nut, and close the mould together, & so make three or foure walnuts.[4]

* Searced=sifted.

Ingredients:
225 g / 8 oz marzipan or sugar paste
2 tsps cinnamon
tiny biscuits or raisins
strips of paper with lines of poetry written on them

Method: Make a mould of wood or plaster of Paris (which was invented in Paris around the fifteenth century). I bought a walnut and broke the shell along the joint, oiled each half with almond oil, and made a mould of each with plaster of Paris, then let them both set. If you don't have plaster of Paris, all is not lost – you can mould the marzipan or sugar paste with your hands to make it look like a walnut.

Mix the marzipan or sugar paste with cinnamon to make it brown like a real walnut. Roll it out and cut it to fit your mould, using a dusting of icing sugar on the mould so that the mixture doesn't stick to it.

After this, you can fill the 'walnut' with sweet treats, or rhymes

Food from the seventeenth century Edible Exhibition, with 'Walnut surprises' in the foreground.

such as this verse attributed to the English composer Thomas Morley (c.1558–1602): *'All things invite us, Now to delight us. Hence, care, be packing! No mirth be lacking! Let spare no treasure, To live in pleasure.'*

The recipe that follows is from Gervase Markham's manual written in 1615, *The English Huswife*. It is for Banbury cakes, nutritious all-in-one snacks, combining currants and spices all wrapped up in a portable pastry package, said to have been made first at the end of the sixteenth century in Banbury, Oxfordshire, and still made there today. When the recipes were distributed in Oriel for the seventeenth century Edible Exhibition, one of the staff members lived in Banbury, and was eager to make the cakes for which her town was known.

BANBURY CAKE

To make a very good Banbury Cake, take 4 pounds of Currants and wash and pick them very clean, and dry them in a cloth; then take

3 Eggs, and put away 1 yolk, and beat them, and strain them with Barm,* putting thereto Cloves, Mace, Cinnamon, and Nutmegs, then take a pint of Cream, and as much mornings milk, and set it on the fire till the cold be taken away; then take Flour, and put in good store of cold butter and sugar; then put in your eggs, barm, and meal, and work them all together an hour or more; then save a part of the paste, and the rest break in pieces, and work in your Currants; which done, mold your cake of whatever quantity you please, and then with that paste which hath not any Currants, cover it very thin, both underneath and aloft. And so bake according to bigness.[5]

* Barm refers to natural yeast barm from the froth on the top of malt liquors.

Ingredients:
75 ml / 3 fl oz warm ale (at room temperature)
2 tsps dried yeast
1 medium egg
110g / 4 oz / ½ cup / butter
325 g / 12 oz / 1 ½ cups strong white flour
110 g / 4 oz / ½ cup wholemeal flour
75 g / 3 oz dark brown sugar
1 tsp salt
75 ml / 3 fl oz double cream
75 ml / 3 fl oz milk
1 tsp each of cinnamon, mace, cloves and nutmeg
450 g / 1 lb / 2 cups currants

Method: Beat the ale, yeast and egg yolk in a bowl and leave for 30 minutes. In another bowl, rub together all the flour and salt, 75 g / 3 oz of the butter and 25 g / 1 oz of the sugar. Warm the cream, milk and half a teaspoon of each spice in a pan, then pour this and the yeast mixture into the flour. Mix to a soft dough, knead lightly, cover, and leave for an hour.

Mix 250 g / 9 oz of the dough with 25 g / 1 oz butter, 50 g / 2 oz sugar, the rest of the spices, and a third of the currants. Stir in the remaining currants. Roll half the remaining dough very thin (3 mm /

⅛ in, ideally), cut into eight equal pieces, place a tablespoon of the currant mixture in the centre and stretch the dough around it. Dampen the edges of the dough, and seal very carefully together. Repeat with the remaining dough. Gently roll each cake seam-side down into a 1.5 cm / ⅝ in thick oval, place on trays lined with baking paper, brush with beaten egg white, slash the tops and bake at 220 ºC / 425 ºF / gas mark 7 for 15 minutes.

Notes: If you use a little ale as well as yeast in this dish it contributes to the authenticity of the flavour. It is important to make the pastry for the cakes as thin as possible, and to seal the edges of the individual cakes well, or they will come apart in the oven.

The next two recipes come from John Evelyn (1620-1706), who was an English writer, gardener and diarist. However many new cookery ideas came along, many old favourites remained, and John Evelyn gives a new twist to this ancient recipe for cheesecakes, as he very carefully tells us how to make what we now call 'puff pastry', probably first made in France. Puff pastry is made from dough which has been rolled and folded several times, with butter or similar fat incorporated at each rolling, and forming a rich light flaky texture when baked.[6]

CHEESECAKES

Take a quart of Creame sett it on the fire and take 12 egges, and two yolkes, beat them very well put them into the skillet to the Cream, stirring it continually till it Curdles then take it off and put it into an earthen pan or silver bason, and putt to it whilst it is hott a quarter of a pound of Currans plumpt, halfe a quarter of Butter, a quarter of Sugar, and a nutmeg sliced thin, for the Last take a quart of the finest flower, and as much Cold water as will make it paste, then pull it severall tymes in Little Pieces, and beate it every tyme with a rowling pin, then divide your paste into six parts roulle them out very thin and cutt them round and lay little pieces of butter round about them, then turne them up once againe, and doe the like, then turne them up and put in the mesur they must be baked pale, if you make them right it will make just six. Lady Hattons.[7]

Puff pastry ingredients:
110 g / 4 oz plain flour, plus extra for rolling out
110 g / 4 oz strong white bread flour
½ tsp fine salt
250 g / 9 oz cold unsalted butter
150 ml / ¼ pint ice-cold water

Puff pastry method: Sift the flours and salt together into a large mixing bowl, then put the bowl in the fridge for a few minutes to chill. Cut the butter into small cubes. Stir the butter into the bowl with a butter knife until each piece is well coated with flour. Pour in the water, then use your hands to bring the dough together before putting it on a board or other work surface. Roll the dough into a flat smooth shape without kneading it. Wrap the dough in cling film then chill it in the fridge for 15 minutes.

Lightly flour the work surface and the pastry. Roll out the pastry in one direction until it is 1 cm / ⅜ in thick and measures 45 x 15 cm / 18 x 6 in. Keep the sides and top and bottom edges as straight as possible.

Fold the bottom third of the pastry up, then the top third down, to make a block about 15 x 15 cm / 6 x 6 in. Turn the dough so that its open edge is facing to the right. Press the edges of the pastry together with the rolling pin.

Roll out and fold the pastry again, repeating this at least four times to make a smooth layered dough. If you have time, cover and chill the pastry for 30 minutes after the second time of rolling to keep it cold.

Chill the pastry in the fridge for at least two hours, or overnight (if you have time), before using it. The reason for this is that when very cold butter melts in the oven, it leaves air pockets between the thin pastry layers after they have firmed up, which means you get many crisp, flaky layers, and that's what you want. The evaporating of water in the butter will create steam, which helps to 'puff' the pastry.

Roll it out to about 3 mm / ⅛ in thick, and cook it at 200 ºC / 400 ºF / gas mark 6 for about 30 minutes.

This puff pastry recipe makes 500 g / 1 lb 2oz of pastry, perfect for 6 mini flan cases of 6 cm / 3 in each or 24 small tart cases. The uncooked pastry can be frozen for up to one month before using.

Filling ingredients:
3 egg yolks
225 g / 8 oz / 1 cup ricotta
3 tsps rosewater
2 tbsps currants
3 oz butter
3 tbsps sugar
nutmeg, grated (to taste)
ground mace for dusting on top (optional)

Method: Roll your puff pastry into a pastry case about 3 mm / ⅛ in thick and bake it at 220 ºC / 425 ºF / gas mark 7 for 10 minutes. Let cool. Place the cheese curd and softened butter in a bowl and blend well. Add the egg yolks, one at a time, beating them well into the mixture. Add the rosewater, sugar, currants and nutmeg to the mix and beat well. Pour the mixture into the prepared flan/tart cases and bake at 180 ºC / 350 ºF / gas mark 4 for 40-45 minutes or until they rise a little and are set and brown on top. Dust with ground mace if desired.

Notes: There is no shame in using a good bought puff pastry if you do not want to make it up yourself. It does take a lot of time, so if you buy the puff pastry, you save time and also are assured of a good result. The knack with pastry is always to keep the ingredients cold.

The next recipe is also from John Evelyn, and is for a popular recipe of the time – Taffeta or Taffety tarts (apple tarts). Taffeta was a silk material, but there is no obvious reason why the tarts are called by that name. It could be that the smooth topping looks like folds in fabric, or it could refer to changeable taffeta, where the warp and woof are of two different colours. I particularly liked John Evelyn's description of the apple slices being made into round 'slates' as if for a roof.

Taffeta Tarts

Boyle your water, and let it be coole, then take a quart of verie fine flower, and foure yolkes of egges, the skinnes being cleane taken away, and half a quarter of a pound of butter, melted, and a litle salt; make it into a reasonable Stiffe paste. This quantitie of paste will make ten tarts, a pound of sugar divided into ten parts will be enough, then take apples either Paremains, or Pippins, sliced verie thin, and lay'd in your tarts like slateing of houses with round Slates, then bake them in a temperat oven, which you must trie by throwing flower into the oven, and if the flower sparkle it is too hott, if it onely browne then sett in your Tarts, which must stay in the Oven till they have done boiling and be sure the oven lid be not sett up.[8]

Ingredients:
Shortcrust pastry for 20 cm / 8 in tart (see pages 27-8 for ingredients and method), *or* roll out and cut into approximately 2 dozen rounds for tarts.
6 medium-sized apples (pearmains, pippins, Granny Smith or other firm apple)
3 tbsps unsalted butter
100 g / 3 ½ oz / ½ cup white sugar
½ tsp lemon juice
½ tsp cinnamon, divided into ten parts (optional)

Method for bottom layer of apples: Peel, core and slice 3 of the apples. In a large pan, melt 1 tablespoon of unsalted butter and stir in 3 tablespoons of the sugar, the lemon juice and ¼ teaspoon of cinnamon if wished. Add the apples, and cook over a moderate heat for about 10 minutes until the apples are soft. Gently mash the apples until most of the liquid has evaporated. Remove from the heat and let cool.

Method for top layer: Peel, core and cut the apples, and use a small round cutter to cut the thin slices into 'slates' so that you can lay these on top of the mixture. Put a small spoonful of the mashed apple mixture into each tart, then cover this with the apple 'slates'. Brush the tarts with 2 tablespoons of the melted butter. Bake for 25-30 minutes at 180 ºC / 350 ºF / gas mark 4.

Notes: These apple tarts taste good cold or hot. I added cinnamon to the mix to give it a bit more flavour, but it was the texture and appearance of the tarts which really attracted people to them.

French cooking was beginning to be admired at this time, and English professional chefs like Robert May trained in France before returning to work in England. Robert May brought French techniques back with him and published *The Accomplisht Cook or the Art and Mystery of Cooking* in 1660. The recipe we included for the Edible Exhibition was a surprising mixture of spinach and almond paste – we couldn't resist trying it, and it was enjoyed as much for the novelty value of the ingredients as for its quality.

SPINAGE IN PASTE BAKED

[Take some young spinage, and put it in boiling hot fair water, having boil'd two or three walms...] being tender boil'd, drain it in a cullender, chop it small, and strain it with half a pound of almond-paste, three or four yolks of eggs, half a grain of musk, three or four spoonfuls of cream, a quartern of fine sugar, and a little salt; then bake it on a sheet of paste on a dish without a cover, in a very soft oven, being fine and green baked, stick it with preserved barberries, or strow on red and white biskets, or red and white muscedines, and scrape on fine sugar.[9]

[Translation: Spinach baked in paste. [Take some young spinach, and put it in boiling hot spring water, having given it two or three spells of boiling (walms),] being boiled tender, drain it in a colander, chop it up finely, and strain it together with half a pound of almond-paste, three or four yolks of eggs, half a grain of musk, three or four spoonfuls of cream, a quarter [of a pound] of fine sugar, and a little salt; then bake it on a sheet of paste on a dish without a cover, in a very cool oven, and while it is still fine and tender, put preserved barberries in it, or scatter red and white biscuits, or red and white sweetmeats flavoured with musk, and scrape on fine sugar.]

Ingredients:
Shortcrust pastry (see pages 27-8 for ingredients and method)
280 g / 10 oz spinach, chopped, cooked and drained
1 large egg yolk, beaten
3 tsps cream
110 g / 4 oz almond paste
¼ tsp salt
2-3 tbsps caster sugar

Method: Cook, drain and purée the spinach. Add the egg yolk, almond paste, cream and salt and purée for 1 more minute, or until the almond paste has dissolved. Gradually mix in up to 3 tablespoons of the caster sugar to taste (some almond pastes already contain sugar, so check on this before you add the full amount). Simmer the mixture over very low heat, stirring frequently, for 15 minutes, or until very thick.

Preheat the oven to 180 °C / 350 °F / gas mark 4. Roll out the dough to 3 mm / ⅛ in thick on a floured work surface and cut 36 circles of 5 cm / 2 in across, and instead of using biscuits or sweetmeats as a topping, cut 36 pastry shapes e.g. diamonds or leaves, measuring about 2.5 cm / 1 in (half the circumference of the circles). Spread about 1 tablespoon of the spinach mixture onto each circle and top with a cutout shape. Bake on a lightly greased baking sheet for 20 minutes.

Notes: Make sure the spinach is very well drained, and that it does not burn onto the pan while cooking. The spinach lends these tarts a delicate flavour, and guests could hardly believe that it was one of the ingredients. The almond paste combines perfectly with it to make a sophisticated taste experience. It is possible to get musk for baking from cook shops, in order to add the grain of musk specified, but I did not add this ingredient.

The next recipe is for biscuits variously called 'jumbles', 'jumballs', 'jumbals' or in this case 'jambals'. They were also known as 'Knot Biscuits', because they could be twisted together and formed into intricate knots before they were baked. The term 'jumble' comes from Latin *gemellus* or Old French *jumeaux* meaning 'twins'. In the sixteenth and seventeenth centuries, 'gimmal' rings (from the same Latin root) were popular in Britain and Europe, and this could have given rise to the name of the biscuits. The gimmal rings, also known as 'joint rings', had two or three hoops or links that fit together to form one complete ring and were often used as betrothal rings.[10] This design is also seen in Elizabethan knot gardens.

Recipes for jumbles varied widely. Some jumbles, such as those from Robert May's *The Accomplisht Cook* below, are large pretzel-like confections made using the yolks of eggs flavoured with aniseed and rosewater which are boiled in water and then baked. Other recipes call for egg whites rather than yolks, and their consistency is much like an early meringue or macaroon. This 'macaroon' variety is included later on from Lady Anne Blencowe's kitchen.

To Make Jambals

Take a pint of fine wheat flour, the yolks of three or four new laid eggs, three or four spoonfuls of sweet cream, a few anniseeds, and some cold butter, make it into paste, and roul it into long rouls, as big as a little arrow, make them into divers knots, then boil them in fair water like simnels;* bake them, and being baked, box them and keep them in a stove. Thus you may use them, and keep them all the year.[11]

* 'Simnels' refer to rich fruit breads called Simnel cakes. The name comes from the Latin *simila*, which was the whitest and finest flour you could get. Like these jumbles, the simnel cakes were boiled first before being baked, and were made and presented by daughters to their mothers on Mothering Sunday in Lent. Unfortunately, there are no early recipes for simnel cakes that I have been able to locate. In later centuries, the cakes were decorated with 11 marzipan balls representing the 12 apostles minus Judas, and were eaten at Easter rather than in Lent.

Ingredients:
50g / 2 oz cold butter
75g / 3 oz sugar
4 tsps single cream
3 egg yolks
1 tsp anise seeds
175g / 6 oz flour
1 tsp ground mace

Method: Pre-heat the oven to 180 ºC / 350 ºF / gas mark 4. Put the anise seeds into a mortar and bruise them a little and then add them to the flour and mix together in a bowl. Rub in the butter until it is like breadcrumbs then stir in the egg yolks and cream until combined into a stiff dough.

Take walnut-sized pieces of dough, and make them into long pencil-thin rolls, and twist them into knots. Bring a large saucepan of water to a vigorous boil and carefully put the jumbles in the boiling water with a slotted spoon. Boil them for just 1 minute, and then take them out and put them on a baking tray lined with baking paper. Bake for 20-25 minutes or until they are golden brown. Remove the jumbles from the sheet and put them on a rack to cool.

Notes: It is sometimes difficult to roll the dough for these biscuits, but if you persist, and press down on the dough to get the air bubbles out, the jumbles will look very decorative. If you want to go straight to the baking stage instead of boiling the jumbles first, this would work, but you then do not get the authentic taste of these confections. In the recipe, the reader is told that these will keep for up to a year if they are boxed and kept 'in a stove', which I take to be in a dry place. I have not tried to keep them for this length of time, so cannot attest to their keeping quality!

Hannah Woolley (1622–c.1675) was an English writer who published several books on household management and was probably the first to earn her living doing this. Her mother and elder sisters were all skilled in 'Physick and Chirurgery' [Surgery] and she learned from them at first, and then worked as a servant, during which time she learned even more about medical remedies and recipes. She married Jerome Woolley, a schoolmaster, in 1646 and with him ran a free grammar school at Newport, in Essex, where she put her medical and culinary skills into practice.

Hannah became a widow in 1661 and began publishing straight away. The manuals she wrote proved to be very popular. Seventeenth-century women were supposed to be adept in the skills and secrets of women's work as an extension of their social role, so Hannah covered topics such as recipes, notes on domestic management, embroidery instruction, the etiquette of letter writing, medicinal advice, and perfume-making in her books. In this way, she connected with the earlier tradition of cookery manuals addressed to women but written by men.[12]

Hannah's first book, *The Ladies Directory*, was published at her own expense in 1661, and this was reprinted in 1664. The costs of her second book, *The Cooks Guide*, were covered by her publisher. Several other books followed, and a compilation of her earlier work appeared in *The Accomplish'd Ladies Delight* in 1675. Many of the recipes in these books were copied from previous works, but this was not unusual. Even today, recipes are freely exchanged, and a large part of their worth is in their legacy.

In the later part of the century, the culinary recipes became more practical and down-to-earth than they had been before. Hannah Woolley preferred simple methods and straightforward instruction, and although she recorded the complicated French delicacy of 'Bisk', she wrote at the end of the recipe that she could not approve of it, and that she had '...here inserted it not for your imitation, but admiration'.[13] The next two recipes are from *The Cooks Guide* and *The Accomplish'd Ladies Delight*.

FRENCH-BREAD

Take halfe a bushel of fine flower, saffron, sage, ten eggs, yolks and white, one pound and a half of fresh butter, then put in as much of yest as into the ordinary manchet; temper it with newe milk pretty hot, then let it lye halfe an hour to rise, then make it into loaves or rowles, and wash them over with an egge beaten with milk; let not your oven be too hot.[14]

Ingredients:
15 g / ½ oz active dried yeast mixed with 1 tsp / 5 g sugar
2 tbsps / 30 ml dried sage
about 30 strands of saffron warmed in 200 ml / 7 fl oz milk and 100 ml / 4 fl oz water (until it comes to body temperature)
450 g / 1 lb plain flour
2 eggs (beaten)
50 g / 2 oz softened butter
1 egg yolk mixed with ½ tbsp milk to glaze (optional)

Method: Take ¼ cup of the warmed milk, water and saffron mixture, and stir the sugar and yeast in it. Set aside in a small bowl for 10 minutes until it is frothy. Put the eggs in another small bowl and beat them until they are just beginning to get frothy.

Put the flour and sage into a large bowl. Make a well in the centre, pour in the yeast mixture and beaten egg, and fold in the soft warmed butter. Mix well together. Knead for 10-12 minutes, adding more flour if the dough is too wet.

Cover the bowl of dough with a cloth and put it into a warm place to rise for 1½-2 hours, or until it has doubled in size.

Knead the dough again for 4-5 minutes, then divide it into two equal portions, taking a little dough out of the rest before shaping if you want to make decorations with it. Shape each portion into a round shape or several long rolls, and put them on a greased baking tray. Cover with a cloth and leave to rise for 40-45 minutes.

Decorate the crust with the spare bit of dough if you like. If you wish the top crusts to turn golden, brush them with the egg yolk and milk mixture, or just cut the dough a few times across the top, or prick with a fork. Bake in a preheated oven at 190 ℃ / 375 ℉ / gas mark 5 for 35-40 minutes, until the loaves are brown and sound hollow when tapped.

Notes: This bread, with its hint of delicate saffron, is a delight to eat. Those who made decorations on the crust with pie cutters for the Edible Exhibition mainly chose patterns of flowers and leaves. We served the bread with quince paste, made from the old recipe from the fifteenth century. This paste, together with smoked cheese, remained a firm favourite to accompany the bread at each event.

AN ALMOND-TART

Raise an excellent good Paste with six Corners, an Inch deep; then take some blanched Almonds very finely beaten with Rose-water, take a pound of Sugar to a pound of Almonds, some grated Nutmeg, a little Cream, with strain'd Spinage, as much as will colour the Almonds green, so bake it with a gentle heat in an Oven, not shutting the Door; draw it, and stick it with Candyed Orange, Citron, and put in red and white Muskadine.[15]

Ingredients:
Pastry for tart (see pages 27-8 for ingredients and method *or* use the 'raised paste' in Chapter Three)
2 eggs (beaten)
110 g / 4 oz / ½ cup sugar
325 g / 12 oz / 1 ½ cups ground almonds

¼ tsp of salt
¼ tsp almond essence
¼ tsp rosewater
¼ tsp grated nutmeg
½ tbsp of cream strained with a handful of boiled drained spinach
   (optional) or a few drops of green food colouring
garnish of orange and lemon peel if desired

Method: Bake pastry case in the oven first at 220 ºC / 425 ºF / gas mark 7 for 10 minutes. Let cool, and mix all the ingredients for the filling together. Fill ¾ full with filling, or make small tarts in individual cases. Put in a 180 ºC / 350 ºF / gas mark 4 oven for about 20 minutes or until brown on top, and garnish with candied peel if desired.

Notes: This almond tart is much like those of the previous century, as almonds were still a stand-by for dessert, but there were some additions. Muskadines are sweetmeats flavoured with musk, also called 'kissing comfits'. Musk flavouring was very popular at the time, and comes from the glands of the male musk deer.[16] It must have given a mysterious taste to any dish that it accompanied, and was considered to be aphrodisiac. The finished dish must have been very colourful, with its green tones from the spinach colouring, the orange and yellow of the citrus peel, and the red and white of the muskadines.

I came across another female recipe writer of the seventeenth century by chance. Sir Anthony Blencowe, who had become the Provost (Head) of Oriel College in 1574, had given some beautiful volumes as gifts to Oriel College Library, and these had been recorded in a decorative Benefactors' Book in the archives. Jack Blencowe, one of Sir Anthony's descendants, asked if members of the Blencowe family could visit the College to see the books and the library. In the course of the visit, they informed me that another ancestor of theirs, Lady Anne Blencowe, had written a 'receipt book'.

Lady Anne Blencowe was born in 1656, and was the daughter

of a distinguished scholar, Dr John Wallis, Professor of Geometry in Oxford. Anne went on to marry John Blencowe of Marston St Lawrence in Northamptonshire, and he entered Oriel College as a student in 1661. As 'Lady of the Manor', Anne was responsible for the planning of elegant dishes for entertaining guests,[17] and she created a manuscript recipe book in 1694 which included both culinary recipes and medicinal preparations for her household. Many of these recipes were contributed by friends and acquaintances, and reminded me of the little *Otterington Hall Recipe Book* of the early twentieth century, which had prompted me to organize the first Edible Exhibition in 2002.

Lady Anne gave her original manuscript recipe book to her daughter, and it has remained with her descendants; but George Saintsbury, a friend of the family, edited a version which was published in 1925. Another friend of the Blencowe family, Christina Stapley, edited and interpreted a more recent edition, published in 2004, which I first used.

The popularity of gingerbread has not decreased down the centuries, although it has gone through an evolutionary process according to taste. Unlike the old breadcrumb gingerbread, made with honey to bind it, this newer recipe of Lady Anne's is made with treacle, which causes it to be fairly hard.

GINGER BREAD

Take 3 quarters of a pound of sugar, an ounce and a half of Ginger, half an ounce of Cinamon in fine pouder. Mingle all these with your flower, and make it up with 3 pound of Treacle, just so stif as will keep it from running about ye board; then put in 3 quarters of a pound of Melted butter, and stirring it well togeather ; then strow in some more flower by degrees, enough to make it so stif as will make it up in cakes. The Oven must be no hotter than for manchets, let it stand in ye Oven 3 quarters of an hour; wash out the treacle with 2 or 3 spoonsfull of Milk, bake it on butter'd papers; mince in also 2 Ounces of Orineg pill, and preserved sittern 2 ounces, and 2 great nuttmegs grated.[18]

Ingredients:
110 g / 4 oz / ½ cup plain flour
25 g / 1 oz brown sugar
50 g / 2 oz melted butter
75 g / 3 oz black treacle
2 tsps powdered ginger
1 tsp powdered cinnamon
1 tsp grated nutmeg
2 tsps milk
12 g / ½ oz candied mixed peel

Method: Set the oven at 190 °C / 375 °F / gas mark 5. Cream the melted butter and sugar together, add the treacle, milk, ginger, cinnamon and nutmeg and mix well together, then gradually add

Gingerbread biscuits made for the seventeenth century Edible Exhibition.

the mixed peel and keep mixing well to a very stiff paste. Stand the mixture in a warm place for 45 minutes, and cut out whatever shapes you wish. Bake them in the oven for 10-12 minutes, until they have firm edges.

I cut some of my gingerbreads into rounds, then stamped them with my Tudor rose stamp, and cut others into tiny gingerbread men.

Notes: I find it interesting that 'manchets' are still referred to as a guide used in directions for oven temperature. Be careful not to put too much treacle in your gingerbread, as the more treacle you use, the harder the mixture becomes.

The second recipe we made from Lady Anne's recipe book was for 'almond jumballs'. This recipe, unlike Robert May's earlier one, uses only egg white rather than egg yolks, so these 'jumballs' are more like macaroons than sponge fingers.

To Make Almond Jumballs
(Mrs Bethel)

Take a pound & a half of Almonds. Beat them very fine with Orange flower and Rosewater. Then (if for white) take a pound & ½ of Duble refined Sugar, boyl it to a Candy, then take it off ye fire. Putt in your Almonds & break all ye Lumps & stir it over a gentle fire till it be very stiff. And when it is quite cold putt it to a pound & ½ more of fine sugar, & ye white of an Egg; mix it well togeather with Your hands, then beat it well in a morter into a past. Then with your squart* make it what forme you please; you may Color some with Chocalett or Cutchaneale. Then wett it with rosewater or juice of Limon; a very gentle oven will Bake them; it is best to sett them on something that they may not touch ye bottome of ye Oven.[19]

* Squart=piping bag.

'Almond Jumballs' made for the seventeenth century Edible Exhibition.

Ingredients:
75 g / 3 oz ground almonds
75 g / 3 oz sifted icing sugar
75 g / 3 oz caster sugar
1 large egg white
½ tsp rosewater
½ tsp orange flower water
several drops of almond essence

Method: Set your oven to 150 °C / 300 °F / gas mark 2. Heat the caster sugar to about 110 °C / 220 °F so that it 'threads' (turns to threadlike consistency in cold water) and is like jam. Add the ground almonds, rosewater and orange flower water, and stir it over a gentle heat until it is stiff. Let this mixture cool completely, and if there are any lumps in it when it cools, put the mixture into a sealed plastic bag and roll the lumps out with a rolling pin. Beat the egg white until it comes to soft peaks, and add the icing sugar to it while still beating it.

Add the egg white mixture, two drops of almond essence, and some red food colouring to the almond paste, and beat until very thoroughly mixed. The mixture will be quite sticky. Spoon the mixture in very small amounts onto baking parchment, allowing room between each one for the biscuits to expand during cooking.

You may put a blanched almond on the top of each biscuit if you like. Bake the biscuits near the centre of the oven for about 15 minutes, or until they are a light golden brown.

Notes: Lady Anne advises you to use a 'squart', which is a piping bag, but I have found that it is best to spoon the mixture on to the baking sheets in teaspoon-sized heaps. By this time, cochineal was used for red colouring rather than the medieval choice of 'sanders' (edible sandalwood). First thought to be a berry, cochineal is made from the dried bodies of the insect *Coccus cacti*, which inhabits cactus plants in tropical America, and is still used by some today.[20]

Lady Anne also mentions that 'Chocalett' could be used as a colouring. This was a very early mention of chocolate, and the kind of chocolate used here remains a mystery. Cacao beans had been discovered by Columbus, and thick drinking chocolate had been introduced into Europe by the Spanish Conquistador Don Hernán Cortés, who first realized their commercial value. He brought cocoa beans back to Spain in 1528 and very gradually, the custom of drinking the chocolate spread across Europe, reaching London in 1657.[21] The chocolate drinks would have been made from blocks of solid cocoa, quite bitter to taste, probably imported from Spain. The chocolate houses also sold a pressed cake from which the drink could be made at home.[22]

Lady Anne lived in Marston St Lawrence in Northamptonshire, and she was not above using local recipes in her cookbook. This is one for yeasty buns, made 'Marston way'.

To Make Buns Marston Way

Take two pounds and a half of flower well dryed, then rub in half a pound of butter; take a pint of good milk warmed, six or seven spoonfuls of Ale yest not bitter, five Eggs yoalks and whites: strain these through a sieve, then mix them well into your flower, and let it stand by the fire half an hour to rise. Then mix in half a pound of Sugar, some currons or carraway seeds, which you like best, and a nuttmeg grated, then put it in pattipans or tins as you intend to bake it.[23]

Ingredients:
150 ml / ¼ pint milk
1 tbsp fresh baker's yeast or 2 tbsps dried yeast + 2 tsps sugar
120 g / 4 oz golden caster sugar
285 g / 10 oz plain flour
55 g / 2 oz butter
2 eggs
40-55 g / 1 ½-2 oz currants
½ tsp grated nutmeg
½ tsp ground caraway (optional)

Method: Warm the milk, pour into a warmed jug and add the yeast with 2 tsps sugar. Set this in a warm place to work. Meanwhile, rub the butter into the flour. Beat the egg and add to the flour and butter, along with the milk now frothing from the activity of the yeast.

Mix well, the mixtures should be fairly moist – with some flours you may need to add a little extra warm milk. Stand the bowl in a warm place for half an hour for the bun mixture to rise. Stir in the warmed sugar, currants and flavourings. Put into bun tins and bake at 160 ºC / 320 ºF for 15-20 mins (makes 30).

Notes: Christina Stapley's redaction works well, and produces delicious buns. Make sure you grease the tins well, or use ovenproof silicone moulds to get the best result.

Up until this time, desserts had been mostly pies, tarts and firm flat 'pastes' of various sorts; or bread made with natural yeast barm from ale (like the Marston Buns above), but it was gradually discovered that large bread-like cakes could be baked using the thick batter made as a result of beating air into eggs. Round baking 'hoops' were placed on flat trays or papers in the oven, and the batter was poured into them to allow the cakes to keep their shape. The hoops could be made of tin, wood or paper, and some were even adjustable. Many cakes made at this time still contained dried fruits such as raisins, currants, orange and lemon peel, and various berries.

When the recipes went out to people to try for the seventeenth century Edible Exhibition, the Provost's wife was Lady Sue Morris, and she willingly made Mrs. Morice's Brandy Cake (a cake she claimed as her own by right!). Although it was not an easy task, she made a delicious cake which was eaten almost as soon as it was served.

There are a lot of things we take for granted these days in our cooking – it would have taken a very long time even to prepare for making this large cake in the seventeenth century. You had to make sure the flour was dry, and the almonds beaten thoroughly to attain the required texture. The lump sugar (which was loaf sugar broken into lumps) would also have to be pounded and sifted, and that was all before you even started mixing the cake! With only a quarter of the quantity of ingredients used by Lady Anne, it still takes four hours in the oven to bake this cake.

BRANDY CAKE
(MRS MORICE'S)

Take four pounds of flouer well dryed & sifted, seven pounds of currants washed & rubed clean, 6 pounds of butter, two pounds of almonds blanched & beat fine with orange flower water & sack. Then take 4 pounds of eggs, put away half the whites, 3 pounds of good Lump sugar pound'd & sifted, mace & nutmegs to your taste, half a pint of Brandy & half a pint of sack & what sweetmeats you like.

How to mixt the cake:
Work ye Butter to a cream with your hands, then put in your sugar & almonds: mix these all well together & put in your eggs. Beat them till

they look thick & white, then put in your Sack & Brandy, & shake in your flouer by degrees & when your oven is ready, put in your Curants & sweatmeats, just before you put it in your hoop. It will take four hours in a quick oven to bake it.[24]

Ingredients:
400 g / 14 oz plain flour
500 g / 18 oz currants
350 g / 12 oz butter
50 g / 2 oz ground almonds
50 g / 2 oz flaked almonds
2 tsps orange-flower water
4 whole eggs and 2 yolks
350 g / 12 oz soft brown sugar
50 ml / 2 fl oz each of sherry (sack) and brandy *or* 50 ml / 4 fl oz of
  brandy alone
¾ tsp nutmeg
¼ tsp mace

Method: Set the oven at 150 °C / 300 °F / gas mark 2. Cream the butter until it is light and fluffy, and then add the sugar, ground almonds, and orange-flower water and mix very well. Beat the eggs thoroughly until thick, and add them to the creamed mixture a tablespoon at a time, making sure the mix is beaten after each addition. If it starts to curdle, add a sprinkling of flour. Then put in the sherry and brandy and mix well so that all the liquid is incorporated.

When this is all mixed thoroughly, fold in the flour gradually, along with the nutmeg and mace. Stir in the currants and flaked almonds, and spoon the whole of the batter into a round 23 cm / 9 in cake tin, smoothing it out with the back of the spoon.

Tie a band of brown paper around the outside and above the top of the tin, and cover the top of the cake with greaseproof paper with a hole in the middle measuring about 2.5 cm / 1 in in circumference. Bake the cake on the lower shelf of the oven at 150 °C / 300 °F / gas mark 2 for at least 4 hours, without opening the door to let out any heat. When the cake has cooled, you can wrap it in greaseproof paper or foil and store it in a tin until you need to use it, or ice it using the icing method below.

Notes: This cake needs patience to make and to bake, but it should be successful if the instructions are followed. Cakes like this are still baked on special occasions such as Christmas, so the recipe has survived well.

I found a contemporary recipe for icing by John Evelyn, so Lady Morris also made this to cover the cake for the Edible Exhibition. This covering is much like the Royal icing that we use today – made with icing sugar and egg whites.

To Ice the Cake

Take a p[ound] of Double refined sugar sifted the whites of 3 Eggs beat with a spoonful or more of Rose water mix in the sugar by degrees continue beating till it is very white and the Cake baked then draw the Cake to the ovens mouth and spread it equally let it stand to harden a litle while and so draw it.[25]

Ingredients:
450 g / 1 lb icing sugar
3 egg whites
1 tsp rosewater
a few drops of lemon juice

Method: Sieve the icing sugar. Whisk the egg whites in a large bowl until they become frothy. Gradually add the icing sugar to the egg whites, a spoonful at a time, and fold in. Add the rosewater and a few drops of lemon juice and stir, then beat the icing until it is white and forms very stiff peaks. Spread over the top and sides of the cake using a palette knife, and stand the iced cake in the oven with the heat off and the door open so that it can dry out and harden to a glossy whiteness.

For this Edible Exhibition in Oriel College, we exhibited Francis Sandford's *The History and Coronation of James II*. This wonderful folio-sized volume was given as part of the bequest of Lord Leigh, an alumnus of Oriel who died at the end of the eighteenth century.

The work was published in 1687, and contains descriptions and engravings of the entire ceremony which took place on 23 April 1685 in Westminster Abbey, including an illustration of the dinner held in Westminster Hall, and a list of the menus for the dinner in this luxurious setting.

Amongst the 144 dishes that were served, the guests enjoyed desserts which are familiar to us from recipes past and present. Whereas some were just described as sweet-meats, others had a more detailed description: custards, a dish of tarts, almond puff, gooseberry tarts, taffata tarts, Portugal eggs (like custard tarts), Turt de Moil (a puff pastry dish containing bone marrow, butter, sweet-meats, cream, eggs, orange-flower water and sweetened with sugar), and a subtlety described as 'a square pyramide, rising from four large dishes on the angles, and four lesser dishes on the sides, containing the

An engraving of the banquet laid for the coronation of King James II (left) and part of the menu (right).

several fruits in season, and all manner of sweet-meats.'[26]

The centrepiece for our twenty-first century event was a brandy cake covered with sugar paste, illustrating the re-building of First Quad in the 1640s in honour of another monarch – Charles I, who reigned from 1625-1649. The hall of Oriel is built with steps leading up to a façade and ornate portico proclaiming 'Regnante Carolo' – 'Charles, being king'. The cake was admired, and then eaten and enjoyed!

Chapter Five

Practicality and Elegant Patisserie

EIGHTEENTH CENTURY

The eighteenth century was one of contrasts, and nothing exemplifies this more than two well-known Oriel College alumni from that age – the celebrated naturalist Gilbert White of Selborne in Hampshire (1720-93), who wrote the ground-breaking work *The Natural History and Antiquities of Selborne*, and who lived close to his home most of his life;[1] and the elegant dandy, Beau Brummell (1778-1840), who was born in Downing Street, admired by Byron, Baudelaire and Oscar Wilde, and who finally made his home in Paris.[2]

In the early eighteenth century, the head chef at New College in Oxford was a man called Radolphus (Ralph) Ayres, who wrote a small cookery book, of which five handwritten copies are known to exist, variously dated between 1713 and 1721. The recipes in this manuscript were dishes which would have been served to the members of New College at the time, and would have been similar to those served in Oriel, so I couldn't resist including his recipe for little suet puddings (called 'New College puddings') in the Edible Exhibition for the eighteenth century at Oriel.

A printed edition of Ralph Ayres' cookery book was published in 1922. According to the foreword, the recipe writer Mrs Hannah Glasse had seen a copy of Ayres' manuscript, and included recipes from it in her own cookbook published later in the century, with smaller quantities given for family and guests rather than for an entire college.[3]

I went along to see New College Library's copy of the cookbook, walking through the College's leafy gardens and cloisters of golden stone, and dreaming of an earlier time.

The cookbook itself is a small quarto of thirty-eight leaves bound together in a single gathering, the binding composed of stiff cartridge paper with a flowery design.

TO MAKE A DISH OF NEWCOLIDG PUDDINGS

Take ye Crumb of 4 penney loves grated, & add to it one pound of good beef suet, shrad small, put to it as may Currans, some nutmeg, a little salt, 4 ounces of fine suger, 5 Eggs beat with a little sack or brandy, you may put in a little Roasewatter if you please, & what Cream will temper it in a pretty stiff paist, so make it in little pudding in the sheap of an Egge but longer, & this quantity will make a Dozen & a half & fry them with half a pound of butter, & Dish them out with a quaking puding in the midle, then pour ouer some butter & strew over some fine suger.[4]

Ingredients:
110 g / 4 oz shredded suet
110 g / 4 oz white breadcrumbs
50 g / 2 oz sugar
1 tsp grated nutmeg
a pinch of salt
110g / 4 oz currants
3 eggs (beaten)
25 ml / 1 oz sherry or brandy
25 ml / 1 oz cream
1 tsp rose water
50 g / 2 oz butter for frying
caster sugar for sprinkling

Method: Mix together the suet, breadcrumbs and salt with the currants in a bowl, then stir in the beaten eggs, sugar, nutmeg, sherry/brandy, cream and rose-water. Knead this with your hands to form a stiff dough. Make 5 or 6 slightly flat egg-shaped balls. Heat the butter in a pan to a fairly high heat, and fry for about 5 minutes until brown, turning once. Serve hot, sprinkled with caster sugar.

Notes: Suet (beef fat from around the kidneys) has a high melting point, and can make pastry very light, but it must be kept refrigerated and used within a few days of purchase. To avoid sogginess and heaviness, it must be baked or fried at high temperatures, and not handled too much or overcooked. Vegetarian suet (made from fat such as palm oil combined with rice flour) can be used as a vegetarian substitute in the recipe.

Suet puddings are still popular in Britain, including 'Sussex Pond Pudding' which we used to have at least once a month for dessert at lunch in Oriel, and a version of which was first recorded in Hannah Woolley's book, *The Queen-Like Closet* (1670).

The New College puddings are very good when they come out of the oven steaming hot, but if there is no means of keeping them hot, they tend to become a little heavy. On the other hand, those who have been given suet puddings from their earliest days in the nursery, or from school days, have a great fondness for them, and enjoy them hot or cold.

For hundreds of years, sugar had remained a highly prized and expensive 'spice' used only in the kitchens of royalty and nobility, but through the eighteenth century, as a result of overseas expansion, the low price of sugar in Britain led to the food containing far more of this sweet substance than ever before.[5] People from the newly rich merchant classes could now afford sugar in its various forms, and it was sometimes used in recipes to the exclusion of other spices.

Along with sugar, coffee and chocolate were now increasingly available to those who could afford them, and were included for the first time in recipes for sweet dishes in Britain. Tea was also imported in large quantities, and 'afternoon tea', accompanied by cakes, became a social event, attended by people of fashion. This popular drink also lent its name to the early evening meal of 'tea' enjoyed by ordinary families.

Women were gradually gaining a voice in the field of recipe writing in England at this time. Rather than starting from scratch with their cookbooks, they augmented, revised, and commented on the recipes of their friends and relatives, emphasising that the food they advocated would be plain and good, rather than fancy and costly, as it had been in the past.

One of the first women recipe writers to advocate practicality, experience, and frugality, was Mary Kettilby, who brought out a cookbook anonymously in 1714 entitled *A Collection of Above Three Hundred Receipts in Cookery, Physick and Surgery [...] by Several Hands*. She had the idea of clubbing together with other recipe writers to present a book that would be useful, and she was anxious to assure the reader that she just wanted to be of help to novices, rather than invading the province of those who had already written recipe books. As she explained in her preface: 'I can assure you, that a number of very Curious and Delicate House-wives Clubb'd to furnish out this Collection, for the Service of Young and Unexperienced Dames, who may from hence be Instructed in the Polite Management of their Kitchins, and the Art of Adorning their Tables with a Splendid Frugality.'[6]

It is worth remembering that the reputations of cooks and recipe writers were built not only on their experience, but also on the social standing of their patrons, so the writers made sure that their audiences knew that they had status and prestige by giving a list of these patrons, or by dedicating the books to them.

Eliza Smith wrote on the fifth page of her preface to *The Compleat Housewife*, first published in 1727: '[W]hat I here present the World with is the Product of my own Experience, and that for the space of thirty Years and upwards, during which time, I have been constantly employed in fashionable and noble Families, in which the Provisions ordered according to the following Directions have had the general Approbation of such as have been at many noble Entertainments.'[7]

Hannah Glasse, née Allgood (1708-1770) became very well-known as a recipe writer in the mid eighteenth century. At the age of sixteen, Hannah secretly married John Glasse, who was employed as a junior officer in the British army, and they had three sons and six daughters.

In November 1745, Mrs Glasse began writing her best-known book, entitled *The Art of Cookery, Made Plain and Easy*. The book was published by advanced subscription in London in August 1746.

Mrs Glasse, like Mary Kettilby before her, aimed to explain cookery in terms that plain cooks and kitchen maids could understand. As she put it in her preface: 'If I have not wrote in the high polite Stile, I hope I shall be forgiven; for my intention is to instruct the lower Sort, and therefore must treat them in their own Way. For example: when I bid them lard a fowl, if I should bid them lard with large Lardoons, they would not know what I meant; but when I say they must lard with little Pieces of Bacon, they know what I mean. So, in many other things in Cookery, the great Cooks have such a high way of expressing themselves, that the poor Girls are at a Loss to know what they mean...'[8]

The consistent popularity of *The Art of Cookery Made Plain and Easy*, resulting in over twenty editions being issued, with facsimile reprints still available today, shows the impact of Mrs Glasse's cookbook on the eighteenth-century table. Her down-to-earth advice, careful organization, and plain language provided a helpful resource in many eighteenth-century kitchens, but before the second edition appeared in 1747, Hannah's husband died, and in 1754, she became bankrupt, and was forced to auction the copyright for *The Art of Cookery*.[9]

The early editions of the book were published anonymously 'by a lady'. Only in later editions did Hannah Glasse identify herself, with the autograph 'H. Glasse' printed in facsimile on the first page, and her full name was first listed as author only in 1778 – eight years after her death. Hannah Glasse's other books – *The Compleat Confectioner* (1755), and *The Servant's Directory* (1760), which she helped to compile, did not become nearly as successful as this major book.

Hannah Glasse's recipes are certainly easy to understand, and she gives quantities and helpful directions throughout. I think of these Portugal cakes as being the earliest kind of cupcake. They were probably named Portugal cakes because the sack (or sherry) usually came from Portugal. Notice that the recipe mentions that if they are made without currants, these little cakes will 'keep Half a Year'. This was very important to a busy housewife, especially in those days without a fridge.

PORTUGAL CAKES

MIX into a Pound of fine Flour, a Pound of Loaf Sugar beat and sifted, then rub it into a Pound of pure sweet Butter till it is thick like grated *white Bread, then put to it two Spoonfuls of Rose Water, two of Sack,* ten Eggs, whip them very well with a Whisk, then mix into it eight Ounces of Currants, mix'd all well together; butter the Tin Pans, fill them but Half full and bake them; if made without currants they'll keep Half a Year; add a Pound of Almonds blanched and beat with Rose Water as above, and leave out the Flour. These are another Sort, and better.*[10]

* Sack=sherry.

Ingredients:
225 g / 8 oz / 1 cup unsalted butter, at room temperature, plus more for the pan
225 g / 8 oz / 1 cup plain flour or almond flour
225 g / 8 oz / 1 cup sugar, plus more for sprinkling
a pinch of salt
1 tsp rose water
1 tbsp sherry (you could substitute orange juice)
4 eggs
110 g / 4 oz / ½ cup currants

Method: Preheat the oven to 180 ºC / 350 ºF / Gas 4. Grease a twelve-cup cupcake tray or a twenty-four cup mini muffin tray with a little butter.

Combine the flour and sugar in a bowl, and then mix in the butter until the mixture looks like breadcrumbs. Add the rosewater and sherry. Beat the eggs well with a mixer, and add these to the flour mixture very gradually. After this is well mixed, fold in the currants with a wooden spoon, and then put the batter into the baking tray(s), filling them three-quarters full. Bake for about 15 minutes, until firm and golden brown. Let the cakes cool in the pan for 5 minutes, then transfer them to a wire rack to cool completely before serving or storing.

The batter will make 12 cupcakes, or 24 mini cakes in a mini muffin pan. They will not rise much, so don't worry if they look a little flat.

Notes: If you make the batter with almond flour rather than wheat flour, not only will it be gluten-free, but 'better', as Mrs Glasse tells us at the end of her recipe.

The spiced yeast breads called 'wiggs' or 'wigs' were popular in the eighteenth century, and also at our twenty-first century event. They rise beautifully to become unexpectedly large, and this is surprising to those who have not experimented much with bread recipes. Ralph Ayres' book contains a recipe for 'London wiggs', but I prefer the recipe from Mrs Glasse, made with nutmeg and ginger rather than caraway seeds, to give the wigs (and the kitchen) a glorious smell of spices. The *Oxford English Dictionary* describes the word 'wig' or 'wigge' as coming from Middle Low German or Middle Dutch, meaning 'wedge', described as a 'kind of bun or small cake made of fine flour'. In the past, I have made up the recipe in two ways – the first being to make up the dough into two large flat loaves, each scored across in quarters or 'wedges' after proving; and the second, as in the recipe below, making a dozen or so smaller buns.

WIGS

To make very good Wigs. TAKE a Quarter of a Peck of the finest flour, rub into it three quarters of a Pound of fresh Butter till it is like grated Bread, something more than Half a Pound of Sugar, Half a Nutmeg, Half a Race* of Ginger grated, three Eggs Yolks and Whites beat very well, and put to them Half a Pint of thick Ale Yeast, three or four Spoonfuls of Sack, make a Hole in the Flour, and pour in your Yeast and Eggs, as much Milk, just warm, as will make it into a light Paste. Let it stand before the Fire to rise Half an Hour, then make it into a Dozen and a Half of Wigs, wash them over with Egg just as they go into the Oven. A quick Oven and Half an Hour will bake them.[11]

* Race=root.

Ingredients:
400 g / 14 oz / 1 ¾ cups wholemeal flour
110 g / 4 oz / ½ cup strong white bread flour
1 tsp dried yeast

225 ml / 8 fl oz / 1 cup water or 6 oz water and 2 oz sherry
¼ tsp sugar
a pinch of salt
150 g / 5 oz butter or margarine
1 tsp ground nutmeg
1 tsp ground ginger
1 tbsp sugar
2 eggs (beaten)
225 ml / 8 oz / 1 cup milk

Method: Sift the flours together and leave to stand in a warm place while you dissolve the yeast in warm water with ¼ teaspoon of sugar. Rub the butter into the flour until the consistency is like fine breadcrumbs. Mix the spices and the rest of the sugar into the flour. Whisk the eggs, warm the milk, and when the yeast is frothy, mix all the liquid ingredients together into a hole in the centre of the flour mixture. Knead the dough until soft and malleable. Cover the bowl and leave in a warm place for the dough to rise for 30 minutes. Shape the dough into a dozen flat buns, score them into wedges with a sharp knife, and bake on floured trays at 200 °C / 400°F / gas mark 6 for about 30 minutes.

Notes: The wigs are delightfully easy to make, and have a mouth-watering fragrance. Just remember to give them time to rise.

French cuisine was well-respected throughout the world in the seventeenth century, with the result that French chefs were copied, praised and hired by the English aristocracy. Many dishes are still known by French names, and various French cookery terms are still used widely in English kitchens to this day. From the beginning of the eighteenth century until the 1760s, however, there was an English reaction against anything French, and this was reflected in the outspoken introductions to the cookery books of the time.

Eliza Smith, writing the introduction to *The Compleat Housewife* in 1727, says that her receipts are 'all suitable to English Constitutions and

English Palates',[12] and regretted that in her book she had to include a few French dishes, 'since we have, to our disgrace, so fondly admired the French tongue, French modes, and also French messes'.[13]

Hannah Glasse's preface to *The Art of Cookery* also included a protest against the French style of cooking: 'I have heard of a Cook,' she wrote, 'that used six pounds of Butter to fry twelve Eggs; when everybody knows (that understands cooking) that Half a Pound is full enough, or more than need be used; but then it would not be French. So much is the blind folly of this age, that they would rather be impos'd on by a French Booby, than give encouragement to a good English Cook!'[14]

In the new cookbooks, order was introduced into the arrangement of recipes in the place of the haphazard disorder of the old manuscript books, and comprehensive indexes were included. Ironically, the change was due, in large measure, to French influence.

Another recipe writer who had a great impact on the time was Mrs Elizabeth Raffald (née Whitaker), born in Doncaster, South Yorkshire, in 1733. Elizabeth Raffald's career was very similar to that of Hannah Glasse. She and her sisters were taught to read and write, which was unusual at this time, and Elizabeth Whitaker went into service at an early age, also training to make confectionery. By 1760, she was the housekeeper at a large estate called Arley Hall, in Cheshire, outside Manchester.

At Arley Hall, Elizabeth learned a lot from her employer, Lady Elizabeth Warburton, to whom she eventually dedicated her most famous book. It was also at Arley Hall that she met John Raffald, the head gardener, who would become her husband. After a year of working at Arley, the two married and moved to Manchester where John Raffald's family owned several market gardens.

Manchester was a growing industrial town, and Mrs Raffald took advantage of this by setting up a shop dedicated to providing for the needs of the newly landed gentry. The shop was described as a 'confectionery', but it sold cooked meats, soup, and hand-made centrepieces for tables, as well as sweets.

Several years later, Mrs Raffald opened a second shop completely dedicated to confectionery, advertising among other things, possetts, jellies, flummery, and lemon cheese cakes. It was at this time that Elizabeth started to compile her cookbook *The Experienced English Housekeeper*. Mrs Raffald, like Mrs Glasse before her, offered her book of original recipes by advanced subscription. She notes in the title page that her publication offers, 'over 800 Original Recipes most of which never appeared in print'.[15]

Realizing where her market lay, Mrs Raffald wrote the book mainly for the staff of the wealthy families she was catering for in her shops. *The Experienced English Housekeeper*, published locally in 1769, was a great success, and went through no less than thirteen authorized editions. In 1773, Elizabeth Raffald sold the copyright to her publisher for £1400, which was a great deal of money in those days. It was a definitive work of instruction for fine dining aimed at novices, using basic cooking principles in which Elizabeth Raffald was experienced.[16] In this book, she was the first cook to offer the combination of wedding cake, almond paste, and royal icing, which still remains popular. I have not included these recipes here, as they are virtually the same today as when Mrs Raffald wrote them.

As one of the features of the Edible Exhibition for the eighteenth century we were celebrating the life of the naturalist Gilbert White, so I made the seed cake below, and decorated it as a nest with eggs to resemble those of a swallow, which was one of the birds that Gilbert White spent a lot of time observing in his garden.

To make a Rich Seed Cake

TAKE a Pound of Flour well dried, a Pound of Butter, a Pound of Loaf Sugar beat and sifted, eight Eggs, two Ounces of Carriway seeds, one Nutmeg grated, and its Weight of Cinnamon; first beat your Butter to a Cream, then put in your Sugar, beat the Whites of your Eggs half an Hour, mix them with your Sugar and Butter, then beat the Yolks half an Hour, put to it the Whites, beat in your Flour, Spices, and Seeds, a little before it goes to the Oven; put it in the Hoop and bake it two Hours in a quick Oven, and let it stand two Hours – it will take two Hours beating.[17]

Ingredients:
225 g / 8 oz plain flour
1 tsp grated nutmeg
1 tsp cinnamon
25 g / 1 oz caraway seeds
225 g / 8 oz unsalted butter, softened
225 g / 8 oz golden caster sugar
4 eggs, separated, room temperature

Method: Line and grease a 20 cm / 8 in cake tin. Mix the flour and spices in a large warm bowl, and add the caraway seeds. Cream the butter and sugar very thoroughly, scraping the sides of the bowl. In a warm jug, beat the yolks very well, and add to the butter and sugar mixture gradually, beating very well throughout. With a very clean mixer, beat the whites stiff but not dry. Using a metal tablespoon, fold the beaten whites and the flour into the creamed mixture very gradually. Add the flour very gently, and stop as soon as the mixture is incorporated. Bake in the middle of the oven at 170 °C / 325 °F / gas mark 3 for 1 ½ hours, and then cool.

Notes: This is a type of 'pound' cake. As there is no baking powder or yeast in the recipe, it is important to retain the air beaten into the eggs, so the yolks and the whites of the eggs must be beaten well in order to incorporate as much air as possible, and the flour must be folded in very lightly by slicing the spoon edge gently down the middle of the mixture and then lifting and turning the spoon very gently for as short a time as possible to maintain the lightness the cake will need.

Elizabeth Raffald was an expert in making what she called 'table decorations'. She gave directions in her book for spinning sugar webs in silver and gold, and has a recipe for 'flummery' – a combination of hartshorn or calf's-foot jelly mixed with cream and ground almonds to make a stiff blancmange-like substance. She used cochineal for red colouring, saffron for yellow, spinach for green, and cream for white.

The word 'flummery' (from the Welsh word *llymru*) has come to mean 'mere flattery or empty compliment' in current English, probably because the original flummery acted as a 'subtlety', or in other words, a deception – meant to look like something other than it was. This figurative use of the word only arose in the 1740s.

Mrs Raffald made all sorts of models with the flummery, certainly reminiscent of the ancient subtleties, including eggs and bacon; a deck of cards; fish in a bowl; a desert island, and the most ambitious of all – Solomon's Temple. She also gave a recipe for making a 'hen's nest', with eggs made out of flummery, and I adapted this idea to make small eggs to go on top of the seed-cake after I had coated it in icing with chocolate mixed into it to look like a barn swallow's nest.

TO MAKE FLUMMERY

PUT one Ounce of bitter, and one of Sweet Almonds* into a Bason, pour over them some boiling Water to make the Skins come off, which is called Blanching, strip off the Skins, and throw the kernels into cold Water, then to take them out and beat them in a Marble Mortar, with a little Rose Water to keep them from Oiling, when they are beat, put them into a Pint of Calf's Foot Stock, set it over the Fire, and sweeten it to your taste with Loaf Sugar, as soon as it boils, strain it thro' a Piece of Muslin or Gawz, when a little cold put it into a Pint of thick Cream, and keep stirring it often, 'till it grows thick and cold, wet your Moulds in cold water, and pour in the Flummery, let it stand five or six Hours at least before you turn them out; if you make the Flummery stiff, and wet the Moulds, it will turn out without putting it into warm water, for Water takes off the Figures of the Mould, and makes the Flummery look dull.
N.B. Be careful you keep stirring it 'till cold, or it will run in Lumps when you turn it out of the Mould.[18]

* The recipe includes bitter almonds, but these contain large amounts of glycoside amygdalin, which turns into prussic acid (hydrogen cyanide) when eaten. The ancient way that people removed cyanide from bitter almond kernels was to crush them, soak them, rinse them thoroughly with water and drain them well, as they do today with other foods such as cassava roots. This method has been written down in the instructions of the cookbooks from the fourteenth century onwards, and Mrs Raffald uses it here, in her recipe for flummery. The method succeeds in leaving only pure benzaldehyde, also known as oil of bitter almonds, if it is done properly. Although this method obviously worked tolerably well, untreated bitter almonds are not widely sold now because the risk of poison, however small, is always present.[19]

Mrs Raffald follows her recipe for flummery by giving the following instructions for flummery eggs in her recipe for 'A Hen's Nest': 'Take three or five of the smallest Pullet Eggs you can get, fill them with Flummery, and when they are stiff and cold, peel off the Shells…'[20]

Ingredients for the 'flummery' eggs:
75 g / 3 oz gelatin or lemon-flavoured jelly
110 g / 4 oz / ½ cup of lemon-flavoured yogurt
75 ml / 3 fl oz boiling water
75 ml / 3 fl oz cold water
2-3 drops of almond essence
2 drops rose water
6 eggshells emptied of the egg (if using eggshells as moulds)
½ tbsp oil to coat the moulds (if using moulds)

Note: I substituted ordinary lemon-flavoured jelly for the calf's-foot jelly mentioned in the flummery recipe.

Method for the 'Flummery' eggs: Make up your jelly for the eggs by dissolving the gelatine or lemon-flavoured jelly completely in the boiling water with a fork, then adding the cold water, rose water, and almond essence, and when the jelly is cooler but still pourable, add the yogurt and mix well with the fork until it is smooth.

Meanwhile, carefully cut a small circle in the top of each eggshell, pouring the egg itself out into a bowl, and then boil the shells gently yet thoroughly so that they are clean and can receive the 'flummery' filling through the top. Fill each egg with the tepid flummery through a small funnel or even the tip of an icing gun.

Let the 'eggs' set in a cool place, or in the fridge. When the flummery is set, the eggshells may be broken and the flummery 'eggs' released. They can now be put on top of the seed-cake 'nest'.

Notes: As you will have noticed, I cheated a bit in this recipe, and have given the ingredients for a semblance of flummery, rather than following the recipe perfectly; but I secretly felt justified in this, as the whole essence of flummery is about deception! The first way in which I deviated from the given recipe was that I used fruit-flavoured jelly which is readily available these days, instead of calf's-foot jelly.

I also used almond essence to give the flavour of almonds rather than using ground almonds in the mix. The ground almonds are used mostly as a thickening agent and as flavouring in the dish, but the mixture is strained through muslin or gauze to sieve out all the solid nuts, so almond essence is suitable for this purpose.

The third place where I veered from this recipe was that I used small commercial moulds to fashion my flummery eggs rather than putting the flummery in eggshells, as the hens' egg size would be too big for the cake I was decorating. Quails' eggs could probably be used, but I did not experiment with them, through lack of time. You could also use little commercial sugar-covered chocolate eggs to put in your 'nest' if you wanted.

Another sweet which emerged in Mrs Raffald's printed cookbook was meringue. The earliest documented English recipe for a baked beaten egg white and sugar confection is the handwritten recipe for 'white bisket bread' by Lady Elinor Fettiplace (c.1570-c.1647) in a manuscript book dated 1604. Elinor Fettiplace lived with her husband at Appleton Manor in Berkshire (now Oxfordshire), a short distance from Oxford. Through a succession of inheritances and marriages, the book finally came into the hands of John Spurling, whose wife, Hilary, used the book in the family kitchen for ten years before she wrote *Elinor Fettiplace's Receipt Book*.[21]

For meringues to be successful, highly refined sugar was needed, and the first sugar refineries opened in London in the 1540s. Refined sugar was still rare, and it would have been almost impossible for anyone in England to have made meringue much earlier than the late sixteenth century. Mrs Raffald includes a mouth-watering recipe for tiny meringues which she called 'puffs', probably because they melt like sweet puffs of air in the mouth.

TO MAKE CHOCOLATE PUFFS

BEAT and sift half a Pound of double refined Sugar, scrape into it one Ounce of Chocolate very fine, mix them together, beat the White of an Egg to a very high Froth, then strew in your Sugar and Chocolate; keep beating it 'till it is as stiff as a Paste, sugar your Papers and drop them on about the Size of a Six-pence, and bake them in a very slow Oven.[22]

Ingredients:
White of 1 large egg at room temperature (use pasteurized egg white for safety)
110 g / 4 oz caster sugar
25 g / 1 oz finely grated dark chocolate (at least 70 per cent chocolate)

Method: Line a couple of trays with non-stick baking parchment. Use a mixer to beat the egg white until very stiff. Slowly add the sugar whilst beating, then the chocolate. Although the mixture will soften and become runny, make sure only small amounts, well-spaced, are spooned onto the parchment. These are supposed to be the size of a silver sixpence, which was a useful measure for everyone to know – it was a tiny coin of about 2 cm / ⅞ in diameter. In the eighteenth century, these meringues would have been put in a cooling oven at the end of baking, as they are supposed to dry out rather than bake. For a modern oven, use the lowest setting, ideally 120 °C / 225 °F / gas mark ¼. They will take about an hour to set firm and crisp.

Chocolate puffs.

Notes: Use a clean metal bowl in which to mix your egg whites, and rub it with half a lemon or some lemon juice, as this helps the egg whites to fluff up. Make sure you only put the required amount of mixture on the tray at a time – these tiny meringues will be delicious, and will dry out more easily if small. Although they will usually come off the baking parchment easily once they have cooled, it's best to make sure, using a knife to lift them cleanly. If they are not properly set, they will be gritty, and unpleasant to eat. Meringues have the added advantage of being gluten-free, and with the added attraction of tiny bursts of chocolate flavour through them, they were so delicate yet flavourful that they were all eaten at the Edible Exhibition, and many guests asked for the recipe.

The practical recipe books of experienced housewives were sweeping the market, and for men to get a cookbook into print at this time, they had to be skilful chefs with a good record of making dishes for well-born people, using practical instructions such as the good housewives had made essential.

One of these chefs was John Middleton, who wrote a book in 1734 entitled *Five Hundred New Receipts in Cookery, Confectionary, Pastry, Preserving, Conserving, Pickling; and the Several Branches of these Arts*

Necessary to be Known by All Good Housewives, and advertised himself as 'Cook to His Grace the late Duke of Bolton'. Many of the recipes in this book were carried over from previous centuries, like 'Good set custards' on page 93, which look and taste extremely like the darioles we saw from the fifteenth century; although the succeeding recipe for 'Custard in cups' contains an eighteenth-century twist, in that the custards are placed in the oven in 'Coffee-Cups' instead of pastry cases.

William Gelleroy, writing *The London Cook, or the Whole Art of Cookery Made Easy and Familiar* in 1762, was also bold enough to compete with the women authors, although he stresses on the title page and in the preface that his are 'improved and practical receipts', and that he had been the chef to the Duchess of Argyle and was now the chef to the Lord Mayor of London.

Translations of French cookbooks, especially those of the great French chefs Menon and François Marin (both active in the mid eighteenth century) began to appear later in the century. The books were full of new ideas for sauces and elegant ways of making patisserie which were to change English fashions and tastes.

In 1767, Bernard Clermont, chef in the kitchen of the fourth Earl of Abingdon, published a cookbook under the title of *The Art of Modern Cookery Displayed*, which stated on the title page that it had been translated from Menon's *Les Soupers de la Cour, ou La Cuisine Reformée* ('Suppers of the Court, or Cookery Reformed').

The second English edition of 1769 had the same contents as the first but the title was changed to *The Professed Cook, or, the Modern Art of Cookery, Pastry, & Confectionary Made Plain and Easy*. In the third edition, from which the recipes below are taken, Clermont added a considerable amount of material of his own with Menon's original work taking less of a prominent place on the title page even though the complete text is still present. The book has on its title page, 'By B. Clermont Who has been many Years Clerk of the Kitchen in some of the first Families of this Kingdom, and lately to the Right Hon. the Earl of Abingdon.'[23]

The Earl of Abingdon for whom Bernard Clermont made his recipes was Willoughby Bertie, the fourth Earl of Abingdon (1740–1799). He was educated at Westminster School and at Magdalen College, Oxford. During the 1760s he travelled extensively on the continent, as many noblemen did in those days, taking what is now referred to as 'The Grand Tour'.

In 1761, Abingdon succeeded his father and took his seat in the House of Lords, and in July 1768, he married Charlotte Warren, the youngest daughter of Admiral Sir Peter Warren and Susanna Delancy of New York. Sir Peter was born in County Meath, Ireland, but entered the Navy and met Susanna while he was based in New York. His youngest daughter Charlotte was born and brought up in their large house on Bleecker Street, and later, when she became the Countess of Abingdon, the city of New York named a square after her (Abingdon Square), which still exists under the same name today, and was on the piece of land given to her by her father.[24]

During the 1770s, the fourth Earl of Abingdon gained the reputation of being an eccentric speaker in the House of Lords. He opposed the Prime Minister, Lord North, and he was one of the administration's most vocal critics in his defence of the liberty of the American colonists.

Abingdon was also a figure of significance on the London music scene. He was involved in the circle of Johann Christian Bach, and was involved in efforts to bring Haydn to England. J.C. Bach and Haydn were among the composers who dedicated works to the Earl and to members of his family. The Earl was also a composer, who set a number of literary pieces to music as well as his own lyrics, and was also noted as an accomplished flautist. Some of his musical works reside in the Senior Library at Oriel, along with the distinguished works of Purcell.

The fourth Earl of Abingdon died on 26 September 1799 and was buried at Rycote, his Oxfordshire home. His wife Charlotte had predeceased him and their third but only surviving son, Montagu Bertie, succeeded as fifth Earl of Abingdon.[25]

Bernard Clermont's translation of the French recipes are clear, plain, and easy to follow – most unlike what I expected after reading the complaints of English recipe writers from earlier in the century. I am starting with Bernard Clermont's text of the recipe for rich puff pastry because he mentions it in the recipe for Frangipane Tarts below, but I haven't included the method because it is the same as is used for John Evelyn's recipe in the last chapter (see pages 108-10). It is said that puff pastry was invented by accident in seventeenth-century France.

PÂTE FEUILLETÉE
(RICH PUFF-PASTE)

MIX some fine Flour with cold Water, Salt and one or two Eggs; the Paste ought to be as soft as the Butter it is made with. In Winter soften the Butter by squeezing it in your Hands; in Summer, ice it. Put Butter according to judgment, to make it very rich, and work it with a Rolling-pin several times, folding it in three or four Folds each Time – use it to any kind of Pies, or small Cakes.
N.B. The Meaning of Feuilleté is when the Crust breaks short in thin Leaves or Scales, after it is baked, occasioned by the Richness of it.[26]

TOURTES DE FRANCHIPANE

Italian Tart after Frangipani, a proper Name (Frangipane Tarts)
MIX three Eggs with a pint of Cream, two or three spoonfuls of Flour, and a proper quantity of Sugar ; boil these together about half an hour, stirring continually ; then add some Almond Biscuits, called Macaroni Drops, bruised to powder, a little Lemon Peel or other fruit minced very fine, a bit of Butter, two Yolks of Eggs, a few drops of Orange Flower Water : Use the best sort of Paste viz. au Feuilletage or Zephir; put the Cream into it, and a few bars of Paste over, laid according to fancy, or cut in flowers ; sugar it over to give a glaze, and serve cold.[27]

Ingredients:
Pastry for tarts and decoration: Puff pastry *or* shortcrust pastry (see pages 27-8 for ingredients and method)

Filling:
25 g / 1 oz currants
25 g / 1 oz candied lemon peel
25 g / 1 oz raisins (or cranberries)
1 small orange, cut up into small pieces, with the zest and juice
1 small eating apple, peeled, cored and chopped into small chunks
¼ tsp orange flower water

25 g / 1 oz demerara sugar
2 tbsps brandy

Frangipane topping:
110 g / 4 oz softened butter
110 g / 4 oz caster sugar
2 eggs
110 g / 4 oz ground almonds
1 tbsp plain flour
½ tsp almond essence
a few flaked almonds for sprinkling

Method: Make the pastry and cover in plastic cling film and store in the fridge while you make the topping. Preheat the oven to 200 °C / 400 °F / gas mark 6. Grease and flour two 12-cup cake trays, or use silicone moulds. Combine all the ingredients for the filling together and mix in a small bowl.

To make the frangipane topping, beat the butter and sugar until light and creamy. Add the eggs and beat again. Finally, add the ground almonds, flour and almond essence and mix gently just long enough to incorporate these ingredients.

Roll out the pastry thinly and cut into circles to line the tins, keeping scraps of pastry to use on the top of each tart. Add a level teaspoon of the filling mixture to each circle – no more, or it will boil over. Put a dessert spoonful of almond mixture on top of each tart.

Sprinkle a few almond flakes on each tart, or cut out small pastry patterns to top each tart, and bake for 15-20 minutes until golden and springy. Cool on a wire rack and dust with icing sugar while still warm to give a glaze.

Notes: The main theme of the Edible Exhibition for the eighteenth century was Gilbert White's observations on the natural world, so we cut out patterns of leaves and birds for the top of the tarts using pie cutters. It was fun to put these tiny tart toppers in place.

The small cakes called madeleines for which Bernard Clermont gives us a recipe, are usually associated with the little French town of Commercy, whose bakers sold the small cakes packed in oval boxes as a specialty in the area. Nuns in eighteenth-century France frequently supported themselves and their schools by making and selling a particular sweet, and Commercy once had a convent dedicated to St. Mary Magdalen.

According to another story, during the eighteenth century in the same town, a young servant girl named Madeleine Paulmier made the little cakes for Stanisław Leszczyński, the deposed king of Poland, when he was exiled to Lorraine. This started the fashion for madeleines, which became popular in Versailles through his daughter Marie, who was married to Louis XV (1710–1774).

To my surprise, I found that madeleines made in England were made in dariole moulds rather than the shell-like moulds that we associate with madeleines today. In *An A-Z of Food and Drink*, John Ayto explains: 'The English have their own version of the madeleine, but its connection with the true French madeleine, and the reason for its hijacking of the name, are obscure. It is a small individual sponge cake in the shape of a truncated cone, covered in jam and desiccated coconut, and surmounted with a glacé cherry.'[28]

Whatever its origins, the madeleine has become inextricably linked with the French author Marcel Proust and his novel *À la récherche du temps perdu* (*In Search of Lost Time*). The madeleine is at the heart of the book's main theme of involuntary memory, in which an experience such as smell or a taste unexpectedly brings back a past recollection. The expression 'Proust's madeleine' is still used today to refer to a sensory cue that triggers a memory.[29]

GATEAUX À LA MADELEINE
COMMON SMALL CAKES.

TO a pound of Flour, put a pound of Butter, eight Eggs, Yolks and Whites, three quarters of a pound of Sugar Powder, a glass of Water, a little Lemon-peel chopped very fine, and dried Orange-flowers; work the Paste well together, then cut it into pieces of what bigness you please; bake them, and glaze them with Sugar.[30]

You will need a 12-cup madeleine tray or a 20-cup mini-madeleine tray.

Ingredients:
2 eggs
100 g / 3 ½ oz caster sugar
100 g / 3 ½ oz plain flour, plus extra for dusting
1 lemon, juice and zest
1 tsp orange-flower water
100 g / 3 ½ oz butter, melted and cooled slightly, plus extra for greasing

Method: Preheat the oven to 200 °C / 400 °F / gas mark 6. Either brush the madeleine tray with melted butter then shake in a little flour to coat, tapping out the excess, or use silicone trays (which I would heartily recommend – I have never been so glad of silicone baking trays!).

Whisk together the eggs and the sugar in a bowl until frothy. Lightly whisk in the remaining ingredients. Leave to stand for 20 minutes before carefully pouring into the prepared madeleine tray.

Bake for 8-10 mins, or until the mixture has risen a little in the middle and is fully cooked through. Transfer the madeleines to a wire rack and leave for a few minutes to cool slightly. Ice with icing containing a dash of lemon juice/orange-flower water, or simply glaze with sugar.

Notes: In his recipe for madeleines, taken from that of the French chef Menon, Bernard Clermont does not advise us to melt the butter, and

A plate of madeleines for the eighteenth century Edible Exhibition.

neither does he mention the special shell-like madeleine moulds so well-known to us – he instructs us instead to cut the dough into pieces of whatever size pleases us.

These instructions suggest that although the ingredients are the same, the batter would have to be a lot firmer than expected in order for the dough to be cut up rather than poured into moulds. I experimented with this method, and made up the mixture without melting the butter first, but although the result was a little firmer than the usual madeleine batter, it still did not make up into a mixture stiff enough to be cut into shapes.

I dropped half of the experimental mixture onto a baking tray in teaspoonfuls and baked it in the oven for 10 minutes at 200 ºC / 400 ºF / gas mark 6, but put the rest of the mix in madeleine moulds to see how that would work. The madeleines from this mixture which were not put in moulds were unformed, rather flat, too dry in texture, and, to my mind, unsatisfactory. Those put into the madeleine moulds were better, but not as springy or tasty as those made according to the accepted method which now prevails.

The madeleines we baked for the Edible Exhibition were made according to the accepted method, and they looked and tasted wonderful.

Solid chocolate (and consequently drinking chocolate) seems to have been available in London by the 1670s, and many cooks took advantage of this luxury commodity. Here is a copy of Clermont's recipe for Chocolate tarts:

TOURTE DE CHOCOLAT
(CHOCOLATE TART)

Mix a little Flour and Cream, with a proportionable quantity of Chocolate, a bit of Sugar, and three Eggs ; boil it about half an hour, stirring continually, for fear it should catch at bottom; put it into the Paste, and Whites of Eggs beat up and frothed upon it; glaze it with Sugar.[31]

Chocolate tarts.

Ingredients:
Shortcrust pastry (see pages 27-8 for ingredients and method)
350 ml /12 fl oz double cream
250 g / 9 oz dark chocolate
2 eggs plus 1 egg yolk

Method: Bake a 20 cm / 8 in pastry case of shortcrust pastry or 24 individual tarts. Gently heat the cream in a saucepan then remove this from the heat just before boiling. Stir in the chocolate and cool until tepid. In another bowl, beat eggs and yolk, then pour into the chocolate, beating constantly. Pour into the baked case(s) and bake for 20-30 minutes at 180 °C / 350 °F / gas mark 4 until set but with a slight wobble in the middle.

Notes: Many Oriel members offered to make this chocolate tart – some because of the very fact that they could make something with chocolate at last, and others because it was so straightforward to bake. The chocolate filling is very solid, and ought not to be overcooked, but it would have been a great novelty to those early chocolate lovers!

❦

GATEAUX D'AMANDES
(ALMOND CAKES)

Take half a pound of Flour, half a pound of pounded sweet Almonds, and five or six bitter ones, half a pound of Sugar, and six Eggs, work all well together; form it into a Cake, and bake it on a sheet of paper, well buttered; when cold, glaze it with a white Sugar Glaze.[32]

Ingredients:
110 g / 4 oz / ½ cup plain flour or almond flour
110 g / 4 oz / ½ cup ground almonds (do not use bitter almonds)
110 g / 4 oz / ½ cup granulated sugar
4 large eggs at room temperature
a pinch of salt

Method: Make sure the eggs are at room temperature and preheat the oven to 170 ºC / 325 ºF / gas mark 3. Butter an 20 cm / 8 in round cake pan.

Put the eggs, sugar and salt into a large bowl and beat for about 20 minutes with a mixer at medium to high speed until the eggs are very fluffy, smooth, and pale yellow.

Fold in the almonds gently and gradually (a tablespoonful at a time) until these are incorporated into the egg mixture, and then sift in the flour a little at a time, and fold it in gently (to keep the air in) with a wooden spoon just enough to combine the ingredients.

Spoon into the prepared cake tin and smooth the mix out evenly and gently with the back of a spoon. Place on the middle shelf of your pre-heated oven and bake for about 45 minutes until cooked through, risen and golden brown.

Pour the batter into the prepared cake tin and smooth the mix out evenly and gently with the back of a spoon. Place on the middle shelf of your pre-heated oven and bake for about 45 minutes until a toothpick inserted into the centre of the cake comes out clean, and it is cooked through, risen and golden brown. Do not open the oven to check on the cake for at least the first 30 minutes, or the cake will fall instead of rising.

Turn off the oven but leave the cake inside, keeping the door slightly open for about 10 minutes so that it can cool down slowly. Take the cake out of the oven and wait for another ten minutes before loosening the cake and turning it out onto a cake rack to cool.

Notes: This is another cake which has to be treated gently. If you are too vigorous in mixing in the flour, or if you open the oven too soon, the cake might not rise as well as you would like, but if you are careful in following all the instructions, you will have a delicious treat to share with guests. If you make the cake with almond flour, it will be gluten free.

The literary tendency of the age was toward a greater regularity of form, mirrored in the Neoclassical buildings of the time, which were designed by architects who developed many of their ideas from classical antiquity. This type of architecture is seen to advantage in the gracious Senior Library at Oriel, designed by James Wyatt at the end of the eighteenth century to house a wonderful contemporary library collection from one of its patrons, Edward, fifth Baron Leigh. The two-storey building has rusticated arches on the ground floor and a row of Ionic columns above, dividing the façade into seven bays. The ground floor contains the first purpose-built senior common rooms in Oxford, and the library is on the floor above. In fact, the whole building looks good enough to eat, and when turned into a cake, we can do just that!

CHAPTER SIX

HOME COMFORTS

NINTEENTH CENTURY

In 1801, at the dawn of the nineteenth century, the first edition of *The Art of Cookery Made Easy and Refined* by John Mollard was published, and was a modest success, reaching its fifth edition by 1836. As the title suggests, Mollard viewed cookery as an art – but one that could be practically applied.

John Mollard was better known as a practitioner of the art of cookery than a writer, and had worked for many years in London as a successful chef and restaurateur. In the preface to the fifth edition of *The Art of Cookery*, Mollard explains that '...the language is studiously plain; the directions brief, yet clear; the ingredients apportioned with a scrupulous jealousy of the expenditure, but at no sacrifice to the interests of the palate'. He goes on to say that he is confident that the public 'will not be displeased to receive the receipts for those dishes they have so often welcomed when set before them...'[1]

We used several of John Mollard's recipes in the Edible Exhibition for the nineteenth century. The inclusion of ingredients such as rosewater provides a link between the old world and the age of industry, and the book itself reflects the transition between the ideas and techniques practised in the eighteenth century and those of the new Victorian era.

Cinnamon Cakes

Break six eggs into a pan with three table spoonfuls of rose water, whisk them well together, add a pound of sifted sugar, a dessert spoonful of pounded cinnamon, a quarter pound of butter and as much flour as will make it into a good paste; then roll it out, cut it into what shapes you please, bake them on white paper, and when done take them off, and preserve them in a dry place for use.[2]

Ingredients:
300g /10 oz plain flour
2 tsps ground cinnamon
175g / 6 oz butter
115g / 4 oz sugar
1 tsp rosewater
1 large egg, beaten

Method: Set oven at 170 °C / 325 °F / gas mark 3. Sift flours and cinnamon into a large bowl. In a separate bowl, mix butter and sugar until smooth. Beat the egg together with the rosewater, add to the butter and sugar and mix well. Stir in the dry ingredients and mix into a firm dough. Put it in the fridge for 15 minutes to become firm, then lay it on a lightly floured board, and knead until smooth. Roll it out to about 6 mm / ¼ in thick. Cut into shapes and

Cinnamon cakes.

place on baking paper on an oven tray. Bake in the preheated oven until light golden in colour (10 to 15 minutes). Let cool and harden.

Notes: The eggs in the nineteenth century were quite a lot smaller than they are today – about the size of a bantam's eggs, so fewer are used in all of these recipes than the original instructions would suggest. I cut the dough for the cinnamon biscuits into small snowflake shapes with a cutter, and iced them with fondant icing. Rosewater is not to everyone's taste, so this allows guests to try a very small amount to see if they enjoy the flavour. Two biscuits can also be put together with jam if desired.

Gingerbread biscuits were a development of the spiced biscuits which had been popular across central Europe since the fourteenth century, and were often put in wooden moulds with designs on them. The biscuits were called by different names according to the country from which they came (for example, *Springerle* in Germany, and *Speculaas* in the Netherlands).[3]

Some of the earliest examples of this moulded type of gingerbread showed Biblical scenes, and were made in Christian cloisters and monasteries in order to educate those who could not read or write, in the same way that early icons or stations of the cross were used.[4]

In the Netherlands, *speculaas* biscuits began to be printed with many varied designs, and used to celebrate special occasions, in particular, the feast celebrating St Nicholas (*Sinterklaas*), at Christmas time, a name adapted by people in the United States as 'Santa Claus'. Dutch gingerbread recipes were prized, and passed down as heirlooms from father to son. When the Dutch colonized the United States of America at the beginning of the seventeenth century, they took their recipes with them, and these rapidly gained popularity in the New World.[5]

By the 1820s, the making and selling of gingerbread leavened with aerating chemicals, such as pearl ash, alum, potash, sodium bicarbonate or ammonium carbonate, had become a professional industry in

Britain. Known as 'Block Gingerbread', this dark treacly mixture was usually poured into the moulds, where it was printed with its design by what looked like a carved printer's block, before it was put into the oven in batches.[6] In the nineteenth century, Queen Victoria also popularized moulded gingerbread as a Christmas tradition in Britain.

Gingerbread figures were made in intricate moulds and sold as presents or 'fairings', so called because they were usually sold at the fairs of the period for a penny apiece. Popular figures would be in the shape of gingerbread men or animals, patriotic designs, or portraits of royalty, and they were often painted with gilt, which led to the saying 'the gilt on the gingerbread'.[7]

One of the best-known sellers of gingerbread figures in London was a man nicknamed 'Tiddy Doll', who was caricatured as Napoleon in a cartoon entitled *Tiddy-Doll the great French Gingerbread-maker, drawing out a new Batch of Kings* by the famous print-maker James Gillray. This flamboyant character (whose real name was John Ford), was known as 'the king of itinerant tradesmen', because he dressed like a man of rank who was renowned for his lace shirts.

When selling his wares, John Ford would cry: 'Here is your nice gingerbread, your spice gingerbread; It will melt in your mouth like a red-hot brick-bat, And rumble in your insides like Punch and his wheelbarrow.' He ended his shouts with the last lines of a popular ballad, which gave him his nickname: 'Tid-dy did-dy dol-lol, ti-tid-dy ti-ti, tid-dy tid-dy, dol.'[8]

DUTCH GINGERBREAD

Mix into a stiff paste four pounds of sifted flour, two ounces of beaten ginger, the same quantity of caraway seeds beaten and pounded, a quarter of a pound of fresh butter oiled, a gill* of cream, two ounces of candied orange peel in shreds, two eggs and two pounds of treacle: let it lie for six hours, roll it out into small cakes or nuts, wash them over with a little white of egg, and bake on thick paper in a moderately heated oven.[9]

* A gill=approximately 100 ml / 4 fl oz / ½ cup.

Ingredients:
225 g / 8 oz treacle
110 g / 4 oz butter
100 ml / 4 fl oz double cream
1 small egg (beaten)
450 g / 16 oz plain flour
2 tsps each of ground ginger and caraway seeds
1 tbsp chopped mixed candied peel

Method: Blend the treacle, butter, and cream together smoothly, add the beaten egg, then knead in the dry ingredients. Roll out onto a floured board, cut into shapes and bake for about half an hour at 150 ºC / 300 ºF / gas mark 2.

Notes: You will find that this gingerbread is quite hard, and will take the pattern of a mould very well.

John Mollard's recipe for 'Twelfth Cake' in the 1801 edition of *The Art of Cookery* seems to be the earliest printed English recipe to be found for this confection. These decorated cakes were an important part of the celebrations for the feast of the Epiphany on Twelfth Night, which included dressing up and mummery (or play-acting).

Baked inside each Twelfth Cake were a dried bean and pea; the pea in the left half of the cake, and the bean on the right. As visitors arrived at the feast, they were given a slice of cake, ladies from the left and gentleman from the right. Whoever found the bean became King of the Revels for the night and the Queen was the one who found the pea.

TWELFTH CAKES

Take seven pounds of flour, make a cavity in the centre, and set a sponge with a gill and a half of yeast and a little warm milk; put round it one pound of fresh butter broken into small lumps, a pound and a quarter of sifted sugar, four pounds and a half of currants washed and picked, half an ounce of sifted cinnamon, a quarter of an ounce of pounded cloves, mace, and nutmeg mixed, sliced candied orange or lemon peel, and citron. When the sponge is risen, mix all the ingredients together with a little warm milk; have some hoops well papered and buttered, fill them with the mixture and bake: when nearly cold, ice them over with sugar or they may be plain.[10]

Ingredients:
500 g / 18 oz / 2 ¼ cups strong white bread flour
15 g / ½ oz / 1 level tbsp dried yeast
150 ml /5 fl oz warm milk (blood heat) for the yeast
1 tsp sugar
pinch of salt
150 g / 5 oz butter
450 g / 1 lb / 2 cups washed currants
1 tsp ground cinnamon
½ tsp ground mace
½ tsp ground nutmeg
¼ tsp cloves
1 tsp candied peel
1 tbsp sugar
8 oz (1 cup) warm milk

Method: Sift the flour and leave to stand in a warm place while you dissolve a teaspoonful of sugar in warm milk, sprinkle with the yeast and whisk thoroughly. Leave the yeast mixture in a warm place until the 'sponge has risen' (i.e. the surface is covered with froth). This takes about 15 minutes.

Meanwhile, rub the butter into the flour until the consistency is like fine breadcrumbs. Mix the spices, currants and the rest of the sugar into the flour. Warm the milk, and when the yeast is frothy, mix all the liquid ingredients together into a hole in the centre of the flour mixture. Knead the dough until soft and malleable. Cover the bowl and leave in a warm place for the dough to rise for 30 minutes.

Twelfth cake (centre).

Put the dough in a 24 cm / 10 in cake tin, and tie baking paper around the outside of the tin to the height of 15 cm / 6 in above the tin for the cake to rise. Bake at 200 °C / 400 °F / gas mark 6 for about 30 minutes.

Note that this cake relies on yeast rather than beaten eggs as its raising agent.

'ICEING FOR A CAKE'

Whisk the whites of four eggs to a solid froth, with as much treble refined sifted sugar as it will take up; then add the juice of a lemon, and a grain of ambergris; mix all well together with a spoon, and spread it over the cake when warm.[11]

Ingredients:
675 g / 1 ½ lbs icing sugar
4 pasteurised egg whites
3 tsps lemon juice
1 ½ tsps glycerine

Method: Sieve the icing sugar, then whisk the egg whites in a large bowl until they become frothy. Add the icing sugar to the egg whites, a spoonful at a time, and fold in, then add the lemon juice and glycerine and stir. Beat the mixture until it is very stiff and white and stands up in peaks. Spread the icing over the top and sides of the cake with a palette knife. If it is too stiff to be smooth, you may need to thin the icing down a little with more egg white.

Notes: Ambergris was still used in the nineteenth century. The Greek physician Dioscorides (40-90 AD) mentioned in his major work *De Materia Medica* that ambergris was useful against digestive and intestinal trouble, but people also used it because of its rarity and mysterious quality.

GUM PASTE FOR ORNAMENTING CAKES &C.

Dissolve Gum Dragon with water, strain and pound it for half an hour in a mortar with a little sifted sugar; add some hair powder, * and pound it again a quarter of an hour. It may be made of any colour by adding cochineal, gamboge, ** &c., and formed in moulds of any shape.[12]

* Hair powder contained fine flour or starch as its main ingredient.
** Gamboge=yellow gum resin.

Ingredients:
450 g / 1 lb sifted icing sugar
1 tbsp and ½ tsp gum tragacanth
¼ cup water
1 tbsp liquid glucose
1 tbsp shortening (i.e. butter / margarine / lard)
1 ½ tsps unflavoured gelatine

Method: In a medium sized bowl, add the gelatine to the water, making sure it is completely dissolved. Next, add the liquid glucose.

Now add 325 g / ¾ lb of the confectioners' sugar, and all of the gum tragacanth. Melt the shortening and cool it a little. Mix all the ingredients together and knead the mixture on a clean surface using the leftover sugar until it does not feel sticky at all. Add any colouring, and mould it quickly into shape to add to your cake or to make free-standing sugarcraft. If you want to keep the paste for later, put it in a greased airtight container.

Notes: John Mollard probably used the starch of the hair powder to absorb the stickiness of this gum paste. Starch can still be used instead of icing sugar to roll gum paste, but it can also react with the other ingredients in the paste by fermenting if kept too long a time.

While John Mollard aimed his book at noblemen, gentlemen, and tradesmen, Eliza Acton and Isabella Beeton were writing for a rapidly growing middle class, ensuring that cookery books became accessible guides for anyone who wanted to cook, whatever their status in life.

Eliza Acton, born in 1799, started out as a schoolteacher in Suffolk, but left her post in 1820 to spend some time in France for her health. After she returned home in 1826, she had a volume of love poems published by Longmans which had some success, but then Miss Acton turned to cookery. After spending several years researching her subject intensively, she wrote the book *Modern Cookery, in All its Branches: Reduced to a System of Easy Practice, for the Use of Private Families*, first published in 1845. Later editions were given a shorter version of the title: *Modern Cookery for Private Families*. In common with many other cookbooks before and since, many of the recipes in the volume came from the author's friends.

Modern Cookery quickly became a lasting success, appearing in several editions and remaining a standard cookery book throughout the rest of the century. The book was extremely influential, and Miss Acton established the format for modern cookbook writing by listing for the first time the exact ingredients required for each recipe, the time needed, and the solutions to problems that might arise for inexperienced cooks.

Unlike today, these instructions were written at the end of each recipe rather than at the beginning.

The book appealed to novices, as was Miss Acton's intention. In her preface, she wrote: '[A]mongst the large number of works on cookery, which we have carefully perused, we have never yet met with one which appeared to us either quite intended for, or entirely suited to the need of the totally inexperienced; none, in fact, which contained the first rudiments of the art, with directions so practical, clear, and simple, as to be at once understood, and easily followed, by those who had no previous knowledge of the subject.'[13]

Eliza Acton also wanted to make sure that her readers were taught how to follow the best recipes, from whatever country they came. She realized that for many years English cookery had remained inferior to that of other countries, and wrote in her preface that 'Our improvement was for a long time opposed by our own strong and stubborn prejudices against innovation in general, and against the innovations of strangers in particular; but these, of late, have fast given way before the more rational and liberal spirit of the times…The details of domestic economy, in particular, are no longer sneered at as beneath the attention of the educated and accomplished…'[14]

The descriptions and hints in the writing show clearly that Eliza Acton was a good teacher who knew her material well, and she wrote that her recipes '…with a few trifling exceptions which are scrupulously specified, are confined to such as may be *perfectly depended on*, from having been proved beneath our own roof and under our own personal inspection'.[15] This encouraged me in my own baking, as my recipes were certainly tested during the Edible Exhibitions.

Eliza Acton's next book was *The English Bread Book*, published in 1857, but this serious and scholarly account did not fire readers' enthusiasm in the same way as her earlier work.[16]

Eliza Acton's original recipes are easy to follow, but some of the quantities have to be altered slightly for twenty-first century usage, so I have listed the modern ingredients and method separately in the recipes below, although you are welcome to follow the original recipes instead, and see how they turn out!

LEMON CHEESE-CAKES (ENTREMETS)
(CHRIST-CHURCH-COLLEGE RECEIPT)

Rasp the rind of a large lemon with four ounces of fine sugar, then crush, and mix it with the yolks of three eggs, and half the quantity of whites, well whisked; beat these together thoroughly; add to them four tablespoonsful of cream, a quarter of a pound of oiled butter, the strained juice of the lemon, – which must be stirred quickly in by degrees, – and a little orange-flower brandy. Line some pattypans with thin paste, half fill them with the mixture, and bake them thirty minutes in a moderate oven.

Sugar, 4 ozs.; rind and juice, 1 large lemon; eggs, 3; butter, 4 ozs.; cream, 4 tablespoonsful; orange-flower brandy, 1 tablespoonful: bake ½ hour.[17]

Ingredients:
Shortcrust pastry made with 8 oz flour
1 large lemon (zest and juice)
110 g / 4 oz caster sugar
2 egg yolks and 1 egg white (separated and beaten)
4 tbsps double cream
110 g / 4 oz butter
2 tsps orange-flower water or brandy

Method: Grate the lemon, and add the zest to the sugar, then mix this with the whisked egg yolks and well-beaten egg white. Add the cream and softened butter, and gradually mix in the lemon juice, stirring it in thoroughly. Finally add the orange-flower water or brandy, and half-fill the tart cases, which have been lined with pastry. Bake them for 30 minutes in a pre-heated oven at 170 ºC / 325 ºF / gas mark 3, and allow them to cool on wire racks.

Notes: These cheesecakes use cream rather than cheese, but this means that they have a very smooth texture. The title indicates that they were served at Christ Church, the beautiful college large enough to have a cathedral in its grounds, whose imposing Canterbury Gate is across the square from tiny Oriel.

One helpful technological advancement of the age was the discovery of baking soda and baking powder, which could be used as raising agents instead of yeast. Alfred Bird, a British chemist, and the inventor of egg-free custard, made the first version of baking powder in 1843 to help his wife, who was allergic to yeast.[18]

Sodium carbonate (or soda ash) had been used for various purposes (including bread making) for centuries, and is still used to this day for coating pretzels and other hard-baked goods, but in the late eighteenth century, baking soda was discovered.[19]

Baking soda has only one ingredient: sodium bicarbonate, and it is primarily used in baking as a leavening agent. When baking soda is combined with moisture and acidic ingredients like yogurt, buttermilk, lemon juice, cocoa, or vinegar, the resulting chemical reaction (called chemical leavening) produces bubbles of trapped carbon dioxide that expand under oven temperatures, causing the dough or batter to rise, and forming the characteristic texture and grain in such products as pancakes, cakes, and soda bread. The reaction begins immediately the ingredients are mixed together; but for many recipes, a longer reaction time is needed, so that the rising doesn't take place all at once, and this is where baking powder can help.

Baking powder is 'double acting' – it has different ingredients that create carbon dioxide gas at different stages of the baking process. As well as containing sodium bicarbonate, baking powder includes other acidic agents as well (often cream of tartar), and a drying agent (usually starch) to absorb any moisture in order to keep the powder's additional alkaline and acidic components dry so they do not react with each other prematurely.

With this double-acting powder, some gas is released at room temperature when the powder is stirred initially into the moist batter, but the majority of the gas is released only after the temperature of the batter increases dramatically in the oven. This means that the batter rises for a longer period of time, making many more air bubbles, and creating a lighter end product.[20]

Some recipes recommend baking soda, while others call for baking powder. The choice usually depends on the other ingredients in the recipe. Baking soda is an alkali and will have a bitter taste unless countered by the acidity of another ingredient, such as buttermilk. Baking powder contains both an acid and an alkali and has an overall neutral effect in terms of taste. Recipes that call for baking powder often include other neutral-tasting ingredients, such as milk.[21]

These leavening agents were used more often in baking as time went on. Eliza Acton gives us several recipes which call for baking soda (although she misnames it 'carbonate of soda'), and Mrs Beeton uses two teaspoonfuls of baking powder in her recipe for 'A Nice Useful Cake'.[22]

The following recipe by Eliza Acton for 'Thick, light gingerbread' is quite different from the gingerbread 'fairings' from other nineteenth century recipes. George Read suggests that this type of confection, although it was still known as gingerbread, came from the tradition of *pain d'épice* or spice breads of France.[23]

THICK, LIGHT GINGERBREAD

Crumble down very small, eight ounces of butter into a couple of pounds of flour, then add to, and mix thoroughly with them, half a pound of good brown sugar, two ounces of powdered ginger, and half an ounce of ground carraway-seeds; beat gradually to these, first two pounds of treacle, next three well-whisked eggs, and last of all half an ounce of carbonate of soda,* dissolved in a very small cupful of warm water; stir the whole briskly together, pour the mixture into very shallow tins, put it immediately into a moderate oven, and bake it for an hour and a half. The gingerbread made thus will be remarkably light and good. For children part of the spice and butter may be omitted.

Flour, 2 lbs.; butter, 8 oz.; sugar, ½ lb.; powdered ginger, 2 [oz.; treacle, 2 lbs.;] eggs, 3; carbonate of soda, ½ oz.; water, very small cupful: baked 1 ½ hour.

Obs. – We think that something less than the half ounce of soda would be sufficient for this gingerbread, for with the whole quantity it rises in the oven to three times its height, and is apt to run over the tops of the tins, even when they are but half filled with it at first; or if it were well beaten into the mass without any water, after being carefully freed from lumps and mixed with a little sugar, the cake would still be quite light.

* This should always be of the very best quality when used for cakes. Carbonate of ammonia is recommended in preference to it by some writers.[24]

Ingredients:
110 g / 4 oz butter (slightly softened)
225 g / 8 oz flour
1 tsp sodium bicarbonate
110 g / 4 oz soft brown sugar
4 tsps ginger
1 tsp caraway seeds (optional)
225 g / 8 oz treacle
2 eggs

Method: First butter a square cake tin measuring 20 cm / 8 in and set the oven to 140 ºC / 275 ºF / gas mark 1.

In a bowl, mix the butter and flour lightly with your hands until it resembles fine breadcrumbs, then add the sugar, baking soda, ginger, and caraway seeds (optional).

Slowly add the treacle, and beat well to incorporate it into the mixture. Beat the eggs very well, and add these gradually, making sure they are mixed in thoroughly. Pour the mixture into the tin and cook in the oven for 1 ½ hours. Insert a skewer into the middle of the cake to make sure it comes out clean to show it is done. Cool in the tin when it comes out, then turn it out onto a wire rack and cover with a cloth to cool thoroughly.

Notes: In the list of ingredients in the book's printed recipe, there is a misprint, and the word 'treacle' is left out of the list, with the amount of ginger reading '2 lb'. This is clearly wrong, as 2 lb of treacle is called for in the recipe itself, so I have amended it in square brackets above.

We can see from her comments that Eliza Acton is still experimenting with soda in her baking. She wants to make sure that her readers choose the best quality product, because she has found out for herself that an inferior compound will detract from the flavour. She also tried to mix the baking soda with water, but discovered that this was not needed after all, and is always careful to give us her conclusions.

Miss Acton also mentions that some writers recommended ammonium carbonate. This compound is a salt which degrades to ammonia gas and carbon dioxide upon heating, and is used as a leavening agent and smelling salt. It is also known as baker's ammonia, and was a predecessor of baking soda and baking powder. It is a component of what was formerly known as *sal volatile* and salt of hartshorn[25] (which was used in many medieval recipes), but due to the ammonia given off, may not be as pleasant to smell as baking soda.

This enticing recipe below for German fruit slices was found in a later edition of *Modern Cookery* (from 1855), but not included in the early editions. Modern German recipes for *Apfelkrapfen* seem to indicate that they are a type of fried doughnut, but this recipe from Eliza Acton is not for doughnuts, so if that is what you were expecting, don't get your hopes up!

APPEL KRAPFEN
(GERMAN RECEIPT)

Boil down three-quarters of a pound of good apples with four ounces of pounded sugar, and a small glass of white wine, or the strained juice of a lemon; when they are stewed quite to a pulp, keep them stirred until they are thick and dry; then mix them gradually with four ounces of almonds, beaten to a paste or very finely chopped, two ounces of candied orange or lemon rind shred extremely small, and six ounces of jar raisins stoned and quartered: to these the Germans add a rather high flavouring of cinnamon, which is a very favourite spice with them, but a grating of nutmeg, and some fresh lemon-peel, are, we think, preferable for this composition. Mix all the ingredients well together; roll out some butter-crust a full back-of-knife thickness, cut it into four-inch squares, brush the edges to the depth of an inch round with beaten egg, fill them with the mixture, lay another square of paste on each, press them very securely together, make, with the point of a knife, a small incision in the top of each, glaze them or not at pleasure, and bake them rather slowly, that the raisins may have time to become tender. They are very good. The proportion of sugar must be regulated by the nature of the fruit; and that of the almonds can be diminished when it is thought too much. A delicious tart of the kind is made by substituting for the raisins and candied orange-rind, two heaped tablespoonsful of very fine apricot jam.[26]

Ingredients:
Shortcrust pastry made with 8 oz flour
375 g / 12 oz cooking apples (peeled and cored)
110 g / 4 oz granulated sugar
Small glass of white wine or juice of 1 lemon
110 g / 4 oz ground almonds
50 g / 2 oz finely chopped candied peel
175 g / 6 oz raisins
1 tsp cinnamon
½ tsp ground nutmeg
1 large egg (beaten)

Method: Make the pastry in advance, ready to be rolled out. Boil the cooking apples with the sugar and either wine or lemon juice. When they are stewed to a pulp, keep stirring them until they are thick and dry; then gradually mix in the ground almonds and candied peel. Add the raisins, cinnamon (if wished), and nutmeg, and stir well together.

Roll out the pastry to about 1 cm / ½ in thick, and cut into 10 cm / 4 in squares. Brush the edges with beaten egg, fill with the mixture and lay another square on top and press them together tightly. Cut a couple of small holes in the top of each square and then glaze with egg if you like.

Bake in the centre of the oven for 60 minutes at 140 °C / 275 °F / gas mark 1, then put on wire racks for cooling.

Notes: The slow baking in the oven does help to plump up the raisins and give them flavour. I have added some cinnamon as well as nutmeg, as this is a good combination, and the fruit slices taste great with whipped cream. Eliza Acton refers to the recipe as 'very good', although I think it would have been improved with puff pastry rather than shortcrust. The later recipes of the 1855 edition do not seem to give separate lists of ingredients or helpful observations, and I found that I missed this feature.

Mrs Isabella Beeton (1836–1865) is still one of the best-known cookery writers of the Victorian era. She was the eldest girl in a very large family, and took on a lot of responsibility early in life. Isabella was sent to school in Heidelberg, where, amongst other things, she learned pastry making, which she continued to practise at a local confectioner's shop when she returned to England in 1854.

Isabella married publisher Samuel Beeton in July 1856, and began to write articles on cooking and household management for her husband's publications. During 1859–61, she wrote a monthly supplement to *The Englishwoman's Domestic Magazine*, and in December 1861, the supplements were published by her husband's company as a single volume, known as *Mrs Beeton's Book of Household Management*.

This compendium was an immediate bestseller, selling 60,000 copies in its first year and totalling nearly two million by 1868. A complete one-stop-shop guide to running a Victorian household, it advised readers on a vast range of subjects as well as giving them recipes which were easy to understand and follow.

The book is most often referred to as 'Mrs Beeton's Cookbook', because ninety percent of it contains recipes, many of which were illustrated with coloured engravings. Recipes were arranged alphabetically in sections, with ingredients, weights, cooking times, and even prices all precisely stated.

I inherited my mother's 'Mrs Beeton' (as we all used to call it), and it contains her pencilled marginalia and careful notes, which never fail to conjure up her presence.

It is said that many of the recipes were actually taken from earlier writers (including Eliza Acton) and that whole passages from other books were copied verbatim, but the Beetons never claimed that the book's contents were original. Mrs Beeton is perhaps better described as its compiler than as its author, and editions of the work came out even after she had died.

Much of the success of this book may be attributed to skilful marketing begun by Samuel Beeton and continued by Ward, Lock, and Tyler, to whom he sold his titles after Isabella's death. The popular image of Mrs Beeton as a middle-aged housewife is mistaken. She did not live to middle age, but died in 1865 aged only twenty-eight at her home in Kent, eight days after the birth of her son Mayson.[27]

MERINGUES

Ingredients – ½ lb of pounded sugar, the whites of 4 eggs, cochineal to colour if wished.

Mode – Whisk the whites of the eggs to a stiff froth, and, with a wooden spoon, stir in quickly the pounded sugar; and have some boards thick enough to put in the oven to prevent the bottom of the meringues from acquiring too much colour. Cut some strips of paper about 2 inches wide; place this paper on the board and drop a tablespoonful at a time of the mixture on the paper, taking care to let all the meringues be the same size. In dropping it from the spoon, give the mixture the form of an egg, and keep the meringues about 2 inches apart from each other on the paper. Strew over them some sifted sugar, and bake in a moderate oven for ½ hour. As soon as they begin to colour, remove them from the oven; take each slip of paper by the two ends, and, with a small spoon, take out the soft part of each meringue. Spread some clean paper on the board, turn the meringues upside down, and put them in the oven to harden and brown on the other side. When required, fill them with whipped cream, flavoured with vanilla. Join two of the meringues together, and pile them high in the dish. To vary their appearance, finely chopped almonds or currants may be strewn over them before the sugar is sprinkled over.[28]

Ingredients:
4 egg whites, at room temperature
250 g / 9 oz caster sugar
a few drops of lemon to rub on the inside of the mixing bowl
a few drops of red colouring if wished

Method: Preheat the oven to 110 °C / 225 °F / gas mark ¼. Line two baking sheets with parchment paper. Put the egg whites and a few drops of red colouring into a non-plastic mixing bowl (metal is best) which has been coated with lemon juice, and beat them at medium speed with an electric mixer until they form stiff peaks.

Next, start to add the caster sugar very slowly, a dessertspoonful at a time. Continue beating for about five seconds between each addition, but don't overbeat. When ready, the mixture should be thick and glossy, and if you have added the food colouring, the mixture will be pink.

Spoon the mixture onto the trays, in whatever size you like, but remember that the larger they are, the longer they need to dry out in the oven.

If you wish to hollow out the meringues and replace the insides with cream, the time to do it is when they have just set, and turned a faint golden colour. If you prefer to cook them through instead, and put cream on afterwards, bake them in the very low oven for about two hours, or until the meringues sound crisp when tapped underneath.

Leave to cool on the trays inside the warm oven, or on a cooling rack in a warm place. The meringues will now keep in an airtight tin for up to two weeks, or frozen for a month. Serve two meringues sandwiched together with a generous spoonful of softly whipped double cream, or leave a bowl of cream to the side in order to let guests do this for themselves.

Notes: I used to be apprehensive about making meringues, because the first time I made them was on a damp day, and I didn't beat them enough, and did not wait long enough for them to set in the oven, so they ran away to nothing. Now that I have found that they need to be dried out very delicately for long periods of time in the oven, and don't like to be damp, I don't dread making them any longer! When I was looking at the drawing of the meringues in a later edition of Mrs Beeton's book, I noticed that they had slivered almonds sticking out of them, so I adopted that idea, and made them look even more special.

Coconuts seem exotic imported items, but they were fairly widely available during the nineteenth century, and the white layer of coconut within the shell could be grated for use in baking. I was very happy when I looked in my Mrs Beeton and found one of the recipes that my mother used to make when I was a toddler: coconut pyramids! I think it was the elegance of their design that delighted me as much as their sweet and comforting taste. Here is the recipe for them – and it's even gluten-free.

Cocoa-Nut Biscuits or Cakes

Ingredients – 10 oz of sifted sugar, 3 eggs, 6 oz of grated cocoa-nut.
Mode – Whisk the eggs until they are very light; add the sugar gradually; then stir in the cocoa-nut. Roll a tablespoonful of the paste at a time in your hands in the form of a pyramid; place the pyramids on paper, put the paper on tins, and bake the biscuits in rather a cool oven until they are just coloured a light brown.
Time – about ¼ hour. Seasonable at any time.[29]

Ingredients:
225 g / 8 oz desiccated coconut

110 g / 4 oz caster sugar
2 eggs

Method: Preheat the oven to 170 °C / 325 °F / gas mark 3. Mix the caster sugar and desiccated coconut in a small bowl, and beat the eggs thoroughly in another bowl. Add the egg to the dry ingredients, and stir until evenly mixed.

Take up a tablespoonful of the paste at a time, and form into a pyramid (or you could use an egg-cup). This should make 12 or 14 pyramids. Put the pyramids on a lined baking sheet (or use cupcake trays). Bake for 15-20 minutes until a pale golden-brown. Coconut pyramids will keep for a few days in an airtight container.

Notes: This is a very easy recipe that children can make under supervision, and is very popular with those who like the taste of coconut.

When I was looking for chocolate cake recipes amongst English nineteenth-century recipe books, I was surprised to find that there were none in the usual cookbooks.

Although drinking chocolate had been obtainable in England since the eighteenth century, I discovered that the great breakthrough in chocolate processing technology came only in 1828, when the Dutch chocolate maker Van Houten developed a relatively inexpensive way of pressing cocoa beans in such a way that the majority of the cocoa fat or 'butter' was squeezed out.

Cocoa beans are approximately half fat in their natural state, and this high fat content made the cocoa residue hard to dissolve, so the fat either had to be removed or dispersed throughout the solution. This is the reason that earlier chocolate drinks needed either to be boiled or whipped for very long periods, and also the reason that the filling for early chocolate tarts had to be mixed with egg yolks and cream in order to improve the taste and texture of the confection.

Other technological improvements to the chocolate manufacturing system meant that sugar and extra cocoa butter could be re-introduced to the finely ground cocoa later in the process so that solid bars could be produced, and could be stored easily, to be melted later when required.[30]

Two Parisian companies started exporting their chocolate to Britain during the nineteenth century: the Menier Chocolate Company, founded in 1816 as a pharmaceutical manufacturer at a time when chocolate was used as a medicinal product and was only a part of the overall business, and Felix Potin's company, which likewise had chocolate only as a sideline. These products are mentioned in the chocolate cake recipe below, which I finally found in the women's section of the *Cardiff Times and South Wales Weekly News*, from 30 October 1891.

By the middle of the nineteenth century, this type of chocolate bar was being imported from France, and was first produced by Fry's in Britain.

A CHOCOLATE CAKE

Particularly one that is neither too expensive nor rich. I can, therefore, thoroughly recommend this one. Get some chocolate – I prefer Potin's 'No 5', as it is much the same price as Menier's and of a more delicate flavour – grate a quarter of a pound of it on a plate, which you put into the oven till quite warm. Whilst it is warming beat a quarter of a pound of butter to a cream, adding the chocolate, a quarter of a pound of powdered white sugar, a small teaspoonful of baking powder, and two-and-a-half ounces of white flour, with a little Vanilla essence. Then add three eggs – yoke [sic] and whites beaten separately – pour it into a cake-tin lined with well-buttered paper, and bake in a moderate oven for not quite half an hour. Do not open the oven door whilst it is baking if you can help it, as that will instantly make it heavier, as we found to our cost.[31]

Ingredients:
110 g / 4 oz dark chocolate (at least 60-70 % cocoa solids)
110 g / 4 oz butter (softened)
75 g / 3 oz self-raising flour
1 ½ tsps baking powder

Chocolate cake.

110 g / 4 oz caster sugar
3 eggs (separated and beaten)
1 tsp vanilla essence

Method: Heat the oven to 180 °C / 350 °F / gas mark 4. Butter and line an 18 cm / 7 in round cake tin with parchment or foil.

Put the dark chocolate in a small pan either in a double saucepan or over a larger saucepan containing water. Warm through over a low heat until it is just melted, and no more. Meanwhile, cream the butter, then add the warmed chocolate, vanilla essence, sugar, baking powder and flour.

Beat the yolks and whites of the eggs separately, making sure the whites are beaten to stiff peaks. First add the yolks gradually to the mixture, and then fold in the whites with a metal spoon, making sure that they are holding as much air as possible as they are incorporated gently into the mixture.

Spoon the mixture into the lined cake tin, level it out on top, and bake for 20-25 minutes without opening the oven door. If you push a skewer into the centre, it should come out cleanly, and the top should feel firm. Leave to cool in the tin (don't worry if it dips slightly), then turn out onto a wire rack to cool completely. Top with sifted icing sugar.

Alexis Soyer was born in France in 1810. In 1821, aged just eleven, he was sent to join his brother Philippe, a chef in Versailles, and was apprenticed as a cook. At seventeen he started work in Paris, becoming second chef to the Prince de Polignac, but left Paris in 1831 and moved to England where his brother was chef to the Duke of Cambridge. Soyer then worked in several noble households before he was appointed chef in the newly created Reform Club in Pall Mall in 1837. In the same year, he married the artist and portrait-painter Emma Jones, who sadly died of a miscarriage a few years later.

The flamboyant Soyer was a kind of 'celebrity chef' of his time. He installed modern kitchens at the Reform Club, bringing in refrigerators cooled by cold water, and ovens with adjustable temperatures: his kitchens became a showpiece, and the venue for displays of his art. He was one of the first to use gas for cooking, and invented several gadgets including the 'Magic Stove', a portable tabletop stove, which allowed people to cook food wherever they were.

Soyer wrote a number of books about cooking. The first of these was a small book written in 1845 entitled *Délassements culinaires* ('Culinary relaxations'), followed in 1846 by *The Gastronomic Regenerator*, an illustrated textbook with 'nearly two thousand practical receipts', written primarily for grander households with a large kitchen staff.

As well as being a famous chef at the Reform Club, Alexis Soyer had a social conscience, and could turn his creativity to writing recipes and instructions for the aid of the poor. In 1847, during the great Irish famine, he invented a soup kitchen, and put it into operation in Dublin, where his 'famine soup' was served free to thousands of poor people. While in Ireland that year he wrote *Soyer's Charitable Cookery, or the Poor Man's Regenerator*. He gave the proceeds of the book to various charities, and opened an art gallery in London, donating the entrance fees to feed the poor. His subsequent book, *The Modern*

Housewife or Ménagère, published in 1849 became a bestseller.

Alexis Soyer resigned from the Reform Club in May 1850. In 1853, he published *The Pantropheon: Or, a History of Food and its Preparation from the Earliest Ages of the World*, a massive volume which the *Illustrated London News* described as 'a book of luxurious reading abounding in classic anecdote and olden gossip'. The more practical *A Shilling Cookery for the People*, published the following year, was a recipe book for ordinary people who could not afford elaborate kitchen utensils or exotic ingredients. Designed for more modest households, both this book and *The Modern Housewife* were written around a dialogue and exchange of letters between two ladies, Hortense and Eloise, in which Eloise explained to her friend how she managed to feed her family, and gave recipes illustrating how to entertain guests on a restricted budget.

In 1855, reports of bad conditions in the Crimean War were reaching London, and Soyer offered to go and help without payment. This offer was accepted, and he went out to Scutari to organize the catering in the hospitals there, later going with Florence Nightingale to Balaklava and Sevastopol to continue the work. The field stoves that he had devised before leaving London (later known as 'Soyer stoves') were sent out and installed in the camp kitchens. They were so efficient and economical that the army used them, in modified form, for at least a century.

Soyer returned home in 1857 and soon afterwards published *Soyer's Culinary Campaign*, mainly about his adventures in the Crimea and the way he had simplified and improved the army catering, as well as a pamphlet entitled *Instructions to Military Cooks*. These volumes contained a selection of recipes for dishes such as salt meat for large numbers, as well as a section on hospital and invalid diets, and another on 'Field and Barrack Cookery for the Army'. Even at the time of his death, which may have been brought on by his efforts in the Crimea, Soyer was designing a mobile cooking carriage for the British Army.[32]

To illustrate Alexis Soyer's work, I chose one recipe from *A Shilling Cookery for the People* and one from *The Gastronomic Regenerator*, as these show both ends of the cookery spectrum.

Rock Cakes

Put in a basin two pounds of flour, half of sugar, half currants, half of butter, three eggs, beat well, make them into balls or rock, the size of eggs; bake on baking sheets; a little milk may be added.[33]

Ingredients:
225 g / 8 oz plain flour
75 g / 2 ½ oz granulated sugar
125 g / 4 ½ oz butter cut into cubes
150 g / 5 ½ oz currants
1 egg
1 tbsp milk

Method: Preheat oven to 180 °C / 350 °F / gas mark 4 and line a baking tray with baking parchment. Mix the flour and sugar in a bowl and rub in the cubed butter until the mixture looks like breadcrumbs, then mix in the currants.

In another bowl, beat the egg and milk together well. Add the egg mixture to the dry ingredients and stir with a wooden spoon until the mixture just comes together as a thick dough. Add a teaspoon more of milk if you need it to make the mixture stick together.

Put dessertspoonfuls of the mixture onto the prepared baking tray in small balls. Leave space between them as they will spread out during baking.

Bake for 15–20 minutes, until golden-brown. Allow to cool for a couple of minutes, then turn them out onto a wire rack to cool.

Notes: These little cakes are basic but good, and they are still popular today. The ingredients are easy to obtain and simple to make up.

Soyer's Meringue Pagodatique à la Chinoise (a meringue pagoda in the Chinese fashion) was a *tour de force* whose intricate design is described with painstaking care in *The Gastronomic Regenerator*.

Table of food for the nineteenth century Edible Exhibition.

Although I did not follow Soyer's instructions to the letter, the recipe gave me useful information about how to build any kind of construction in meringue, so I chose to use the same principles to make a meringue model of Oriel College instead of a pagoda.

MERINGUE PAGODATIQUE À LA CHINOISE

Have ready prepared a meringue mixture of fifteen eggs, with which make six rings upon paper, (laying them out with a paper cornet or funnel, in the bottom of which you have cut a hole of the circumference of a shilling,) the three largest to be eight inches in diameter, the next one six and a half inches, the next five, and the smallest three and a half inches in diameter, and the whole of them an inch in thickness, have some of the preparation in a small paper cornet with a hole at the bottom of the size of a pea, with which ornament the rings, laying small fillets of it over them, then with the large paper cornet lay out four other pieces of an octagonal form, (to imitate the top of a Chinese pagoda, which may easily be accomplished if the mixture is firm, as it may then be laid out into any shape desired,) leaving a ring in the centre, making the largest rather larger than the largest ring, diminishing the size in proportion to the other rings, and piping them according to fancy with the smaller paper cornet with which also form sixteen little bells by pressing an upright dot from it upon paper, and pulling the cornet up quickly, making the four largest half an inch in height and a quarter of an inch in width, and making each four a size smaller in proportion; bake the whole of the preparations (first sifting sugar over them) upon boards in a very slow oven, scarcely allowing them to attain any colour; when baked and crisp place them in a hot closet until perfectly dry, when take them out, wet the back of the papers lightly with a paste-brush and carefully detach the meringues from them, which again put into the hot closet until quite crisp, then fix the bells, the largest upon the largest octagonal piece at the corners, and the smaller upon the smaller pieces, by running a needle with a piece of white silk through them, and fastening them with a little boiled sugar or isinglass when upon the point of setting; when ready to serve place the three largest rings upon your dish, filling the middle with some whipped cream flavoured with vanilla sugar, then the largest octagonal piece, which also fill with cream, then the next sized ring, and so on until you have built the whole up, finishing with the smallest octagonal at the top, you have also made and baked a pointed meringue of the shape of half a lemon, to fit into the hole at the top, having it decorated to correspond, which place upon the top and serve immediately, or it would become damp, and eat toughish instead of crisp.[34]

Ingredients:
For the meringue:
15 pasteurised egg whites
750 g / 2 lbs caster sugar
pinch of salt
2 tsps lemon juice
1 tsp of ginger
1 tsp of cinnamon

Method: Whisk whites to stiff peaks, add sugar slowly and add lemon juice and salt, and also ginger and cinnamon (to make it look like stone). Make your meringue patterns on baking trays covered with baking parchment, cook all on pilot (the lowest possible heat) for 6-8 hours, then assemble the construction using melted sugar or royal icing to keep it together, and whipped cream for decoration between layers.

For the centrepiece of the nineteenth century Edible Exhibition, I decided to make 'Meringue Oriel' – a model of Oriel College's first quad, by using a diagram of the buildings to craft a 'foundation plan' in meringue on baking parchment, then baking tiny meringue walls, windows, roofs, and steps, sticking all of these building blocks together with royal icing, and surmounting them with meringue finials. The 'grass' in the meringue quad was made of green-coloured royal icing. It is important that royal icing is used with meringue, because water-based icing will cause the structure to soften and break down.

'Meringue Oriel' was presented at the Edible Exhibition, and later divided so that members of Oriel could eat their own 'rooms' from First Quad!

'Meringue Oriel' on display at the nineteenth century Edible Exhibition.

CHAPTER SEVEN

COUNTRY HOUSE CONFECTIONS

EARLY TWENTIETH CENTURY

The beautifully printed and bound *Otterington Hall Recipe Book*[1] contains recipes gathered by Lady Eleanor Furness in the late nineteenth and early twentieth centuries, and edited by her daughter Mary and son Stephen.

Eleanor Furness née Forster, was born in 1871, and came originally from Adelaide in Southern Australia. Eleanor married Stephen Wilson Furness on 5 September 1899. The couple had four children: Christopher, born in October 1900; Stephen Noel, born in December 1902; Eleanor Mary, born in August 1904, and Frank Wilson, born in April 1906.

Stephen Wilson Furness was an able businessman, and had taken over the chairmanship of the family shipping firm (Furness Withy & Company) from his uncle, Sir Christopher Furness. Like his uncle before him, he was voted in as Member of Parliament for the borough of The Hartlepools (now Hartlepool) in County Durham between 1910 and 1914, and was also a Justice of the Peace. He was created 1st Baronet Furness, of Tunstall Grange, West Hartlepool, County Durham, in June 1913, but sadly Sir Stephen died just over a year later in an accident on 6 September 1914.[2]

Up until Sir Stephen died, the family had lived in Tunstall Grange in West Hartlepool, but then Lady Eleanor and the children moved to Otterington Hall, near Northallerton, North Yorkshire.

Otterington Hall dates from the early nineteenth century, and is surrounded by sweeping grasslands overlooking the North York Moors, which is now a national park. The house itself is a beautiful rambling red brick building with tall sash windows and ornate plaster work. The front lawns and gardens have been made into garden 'rooms' with various borders and water features, and there is a kitchen garden at the back of the house, along with a tennis court, ponds and woods. The gardens still have a unique gallery of yew sculptures, which dates from the 1920s, and is said to have been designed by Lady Eleanor herself.

The family enjoyed their home life, and treasured happy memories of the years under their mother's care. After Lady Eleanor died in 1936, the old dilapidated exercise book containing her recipes and notes was preserved, and when Mary and Steve (as they call themselves in the preface) compiled the *Otterington Hall Recipe Book*, they recorded the origin of the individual recipes if they could. When Steve himself died in 1974, he bequeathed his copy to Oriel College Library, and all of the recipes in this chapter come from this little book.

The first sweet recipe we are going to look at from the *Otterington Hall Recipe Book* is one which carries an ancient name. In medieval times, the sweetmeats known as 'darioles' (or the many other variant spellings of the same term such as 'darrioles') were small custard tarts with a pastry case, originally made in France. The name came from their golden-brown colour (*dorer* meant 'to gild' in French).

In later centuries, the name came to be associated with the dariole mould rather than the sweetmeat itself.[3] In John Ayto's book *An A-Z of Food and Drink*, a dariole is described as 'a small cup-shaped mould in which are made sweet or savoury puddings, cakes, jellies, cream desserts, etc. (which in their turn are called darioles)'.[4] Dariole moulds are still made today, so you will have no trouble finding them if you want to make the first recipe in our selection from the *Otterington Hall Recipe Book* – 'Darrioles à la Duchesse' – a sweet spongy trifle of a dessert.

DARRIOLES À LA DUCHESSE
(MRS DIXON)

Thoroughly mix 4 ozs flour with a whole egg. Add the yolks only of three eggs besides 1 oz powdered sugar, four macaroons thoroughly [c]rushed, and another whole egg. These ingredients should be added to each other singly, and when thoroughly well mixed, stir in a teacupful of cream, vanilla essence, a pinch of angelica, minced very small, and a little mixed preserved fruit. Pour this mixture into buttered darriole moulds and bake in a quick oven.[5]

Ingredients:
110 g / 4 oz flour
2 eggs + 3 yolks
25 g / 1 oz sugar
4 macaroons, crushed (see separate recipe below)
175 g / 6 oz / teacupful double cream
1 tsp vanilla essence
½ tsp of finely cut up angelica
½ tsp candied fruit

Bake in the centre of a pre-heated oven at 190 ºC / 375 ºF / gas mark 5 for 15 minutes.

The recipe above calls for crushed macaroons – these are English macaroons rather than French macarons, and would be made with a little cornflour. You may know how to make macaroons, but if not, here is one of my mother's recipes:

MACAROONS

Ingredients:
125 g / 4 ½ oz ground almonds
175 g / 6 oz caster sugar

1 tbsp cornflour
2 medium egg whites
½ tsp vanilla essence

* For use in the previous recipe.

Method: Line two baking trays with baking parchment, and preheat the oven to 160 °C / 325 °F / gas mark 3. Mix the ground almonds with the sugar and cornflour in a large bowl. In another bowl, whisk the egg whites with the vanilla extract using a fork, until just frothy. Add the whites to the almond mixture and stir with a wooden spoon until it makes a stiff dough.

Spoon the mixture with a dessert spoon on to the lined baking trays in 10 mounds, spacing them very well apart. Gently spread out each mound to make a disc about 5 cm / 2 in across and 1.5 cm / ⅝ in high – they will spread in the oven. Bake for 20-25 minutes, then cool on a wire tray.

Notes: The finished recipe for these darioles is very rich and suits people with a sweet tooth, like the Victorians, who developed a taste for extremely sweet dishes while sugar was so low in price.

Mary and Steve's aunt, Mrs. Annette Bryan, who contributed several recipes to the *Otterington Hall Recipe Book*, wrote some recollections of her own life which were printed in another little book edited by Steve in 1973, entitled *Yesterday,* also in the Oriel collection.

Born in the province of Blekinge in Sweden, Annette Furness came to England in 1887 at the age of eleven and lived at the home of her Uncle Christopher and Aunt Jane Furness until her marriage in 1911 to Claude Glennon Bryan, who was originally from Toronto, Canada.

The introduction tells us that the narrative of Annette Bryan's book 'takes us from Sweden to the North of England, and from thence to London before, during, and after the turn of the [twentieth] century...'[6]

Early on in the account, the author remarks: 'Perhaps one of the great changes to record is the evening meal. In my early youth in the North of England 'high tea' consisting of a variety of fish or meat dishes was served at 6.30 p.m. Cakes of every variety, hot home-made buttered tea cakes and how delicious they were, cut in four and the best part the bottom pieces. I cannot remember if tea was served at this meal; a light tea was served at 4.30 p.m. with bread and butter and cakes and called afternoon tea. Eventually this meal was abolished, replaced by dinner at 8 o'clock. The reason of the change was consideration for visitors unfamiliar with this north-country custom of 'high tea'.[7]

Here is one of the recipes from Mrs Bryan which would have been very popular at high tea – luscious Strawberry Mess, which was served on 4th June at Eton. Nowadays, we make Eton Mess with crushed meringue pieces as well as syrup, but this simple recipe does not mention meringues.

STRAWBERRY MESS (4TH JUNE AT ETON)

Strawberries are picked and soaked in cold syrup. If they can be chilled by placing on ice so much the better.

For the syrup: Boil 1 lb. loaf sugar with ½ pint water until it Forms a thread when the fingers are dipped in and pulled apart. Then flavour it with lemon juice and colour pink with cochineal.

A bowl is lined with strawberries, the centre is filled with strawberry ice cream and strawberries and syrup is poured over all.[8]

Ingredients:
450 g / 1 lb fresh strawberries
225 g / 8 oz granulated sugar
275 ml / ½ pint cold water
1 tsp lemon juice
3 large strawberries, sliced for the syrup
a few drops red food colouring
strawberry ice-cream to taste

Method for syrup: In a high-sided saucepan over medium heat, bring cold water and sugar to a boil. Turn the heat to low and stir constantly until the sugar dissolves completely and the mixture is clear, approximately 3 to 5 minutes. The longer you boil it, the thicker the syrup will be when cooled.

To test if the sugar is completely dissolved, take up a small amount of the syrup with a spoon. You should not be able to see any sugars crystals in the liquid. If you do, boil it for a little longer, then reduce heat and add the three sliced strawberries and lemon juice. Cover and simmer for about 5 more minutes, stirring occasionally, then remove from the heat and allow to cool and infuse for about 2 hours.

Strain to remove all the strawberries, then pour into a tightly sealed, clean glass jar and store in the refrigerator (any clean and sealable container can be used).

Method for strawberry mixture: Roughly mash half of the strawberries, and then slice the rest, soak them all in half the syrup, when it is cold, and line a bowl with them. Fill the centre of the bowl with strawberry ice-cream and the rest of the strawberries, and pour the remaining syrup over all.

Mary and Steve's elderly nurse, Nanna, provided the recipe for Quaker Oats biscuits below. Nanna had been associated with the family for over sixty-eight years and lived in the nearby village of Thornton-le-Moor. What is better than having a much-loved recipe which goes back to your childhood? The smell of these biscuits alone would bring back memories!

QUAKER OATS BISCUITS
(NANNA)

1 breakfast cup* of flour
1 breakfast cup of sugar
1 breakfast cup of Quaker Oats
1 breakfast cup of Coconut
½ lb margarine
1 egg
A small quantity chopped walnuts
1 tablespoonful treacle
1 teaspoonful of carbonate of soda[9]

*Note: A breakfast cup is 225 g / 8 oz.

Method: Preheat oven to 170 °C / 325 °F / gas mark 3. Mix all the ingredients in a bowl together with your hands – you would have enjoyed doing this as a child!

Drop rounded tablespoonfuls of the mixture on to ungreased trays, and shape into biscuits. Make sure they are evenly spaced as they will rise and spread slightly. Cook for 10-12 mins or until golden brown and cracked. You may have to turn the trays once to ensure even cooking. Remove from oven. Leave to cool a little and turn out onto a wire rack. If you prefer really crunchy biscuits, turn off the oven and leave the biscuits in there until cool.

Notes: When I ate these biscuits as a child, they comforted and warmed me, and started me off with a lifelong affection for muesli biscuits – they are wonderful, healthy snacks for taking on a long walk in the Yorkshire Moors or anywhere else you happen to be!

The next recipe is from Grantley Hall, the home of Sir Christopher Furness and his wife Jane. Mary and Steve describe them in their introduction to the recipe book as 'Big Uncle and Big Auntie' – their Great Uncle and Great Aunt, Lord and Lady Furness.

Mary and Steve's Great Uncle Christopher, born in 1852 at West Hartlepool, was the seventh and youngest son of John Furness (1808–1885), who was a provision merchant. All the sons of John and his wife Averill helped to run their father's import/export wholesale firm, but under the management of the eldest son, Thomas (born in 1836), the firm became known as Thomas Furness & Co., and soon developed into one of the largest of its kind in north-eastern England.

Christopher Furness was given unique opportunities owing to the technological advances of the Industrial Revolution, and also had his share of good fortune to help him on his way. Having proved himself to be commercially astute, Christopher went to Sweden as a buyer for the family firm, and made the firm a large profit. As a result, he was made a partner in the company. In May 1876, Christopher married his wife Jane – the start of a happy union.

After realizing that the firm could profit from making use of the family ships for trade instead of hiring them out to others, Christopher bought sailing vessels for the firm in 1877 and started a regular service between Boston, Massachusetts, and West Hartlepool. Differences of opinion about the future of the firm arose between the eldest and youngest brothers. The brothers divided the assets of the company between them in 1882. Thomas kept the grocery business, while Christopher took charge of the shipping fleet.

In 1891, Christopher merged his fleet with the West Hartlepool shipbuilding firm of Edward Withy & Company, in which he had acquired an interest in 1882, and the firm Furness, Withy & Company was formed.

Christopher Furness was keenly interested in making commercial use of new technology. He built Britain's first motor ship, *Eavestone*, and the first turbine-powered vessel to cross the Atlantic was his yacht, *Emerald*. By a series of mergers, his firms become the main employers in Hartlepool, until they finally closed in the 1980s.

Not only a successful businessman, Christopher Furness also served as an MP for The Hartlepools for several years. He was knighted by Queen Victoria in the 1895 Birthday Honours. The family moved to Grantley Hall in 1900, and Christopher was raised to the peerage in 1910 as 1st Baron Furness of Grantley.[10]

Grantley Hall was a happy home for Christopher Furness and his wife Jane right from the time they purchased it. Over the years, they made several improvements and additions to the house and gardens, which still remain in evidence today.

Like Lady Eleanor, Lady Jane was a keen gardener, and around the year 1910 directed the installation of a Japanese Garden, which was the first of its kind ever planted in England.[11] Interest in Japanese-influenced gardens developed from the late Victorian period, but became highly fashionable following a major exhibition in the summer of 1910 at White City, London.

The garden follows authentic Japanese design principles. It features two ponds linked by a stream with large, irregular stepping stones; diverse trees, mosses, ferns and bamboo; and Japanese stone lanterns, one of which can still be seen. The bridge across the northern pond is a late twentieth century replacement of the original which paintings and photographs show was a red lacquered timber bridge reminiscent of the red bridge at Nikko, Japan.[12]

Lady Jane Furness loved art and beautiful things, and filled the house with fine furniture, paintings and sculptures.

The household at Grantley Hall contributed several recipes to the *Otterington Hall Recipe Book*, and this included a Rum Cake. Rum is a distilled liquor from sugarcane products, first discovered in Barbados in the seventeenth century, and quickly becoming the drink of choice for the Navy.

Sweet water was in short supply on Navy ships, and any kept in casks would become stagnant, develop algae, and taste sour; beer wouldn't last well in humid conditions either. Spirits like rum or brandy would keep fresh, taste good, and could also be mixed with water and lime juice to make a drink known as 'grog' which helped to prevent scurvy. British sailors received regular rations of rum from the eighteenth century until 1970.[13]

In most of the Caribbean, rum cakes are a traditional holiday season dessert, and are often used as presents at Christmas. In these cakes, dried fruit is soaked in rum for many months and then added to dough prepared with sugar which has been caramelized by boiling in water. The recipe below is a quick method of making rum cake, and is not as full-flavoured as the Caribbean version, but tastes delicious all the same.

Rum Cake
(Grantley)

450 g / 1 lb butter
450 g / 1 lb sugar (or 225 g / 8 oz sugar + 225 g / 8 oz treacle)
8 eggs
450 g / 1 lb flour
110 g / 4 oz / ¼ lb almonds
110 g / 4 oz / ¼ lb candied peel
450 g / 1 lb sultanas
450 g / 1 lb currants

Wine glass of rum (150 g / 5 oz)
A little black treacle may be used, if desired very dark.
Beat butter and sugar well. Add eggs, one by one. Beat until light
and creamy. Add flour, fruit and rum. Bake in a moderate oven.[14]

Method: Follow instructions above and bake for an hour in a 25 cm / 10 in cake tin or bundt tin at 150 °C / 300 °F / gas mark 2. If you want to make it with treacle, use 225 g / 8 oz of sugar and 225 g / 8 oz treacle rather than 450 g / 1 lb sugar.

Mrs Gregory was Lady Eleanor's sister, and the wife of the Revd Bertram Gregory, vicar of the beautiful Norman church of St Andrew's Grinton in Swaledale from 1907 until he retired with his wife to live near Malvern. The following recipe for coffee cake comes from Mrs Gregory.

In Mrs Gregory's coffee cake, liquid coffee essence is used. This was invented in Scotland in 1840 by chemist T & H Smith of Edinburgh, and the well-known Camp Coffee, another Scottish coffee and chicory essence, began production in 1876 and is still available today. In Britain, coffee essence was widely advertised as the earliest form of instant coffee. Chicory was commonly added to coffee essence – lowering the cost, but also adding its own distinctive flavour.[15]

COFFEE CAKE
(MRS GREGORY'S)

4 ozs. butter	*4 ozs. sugar*
2 eggs	*6 ozs. flour*
1 tablespoonful coffee essence	*1 ½ tsp baking powder*

Beat butter and sugar to a cream.
Add the eggs and flour alternately.
Mix in the coffee essence and lastly baking powder.
Bake in a moderate oven.

Filling for cake:
2 ozs. butter
4 ozs. caster sugar
½ teaspoonful vanilla essence[16]

Use the same ingredients as above, but if you don't have coffee essence, use 1 tablespoon of instant coffee (or more if you like it strong) dissolved in 1 tablespoon of hot water.

Method: Preheat the oven to 170 °C / 325 °F / gas mark 3. Line and grease two 18 cm / 7 in sandwich tins. Add the sugar and butter to a bowl and beat until the mixture is very fluffy and pale.

Whisk the eggs in a bowl, then add them gradually to the mixture alternately with a tablespoon of flour each time until you have used 110 g / 4 oz of the flour. When the eggs have been fully combined into the mix, add the coffee essence or dissolved coffee, folding it gently into the mix. Finally, add the rest of the flour with the baking powder combined with it, and fold it all together gently.

Divide the batter into the sandwich tins and cook for 25-30 mins until risen and firm and a skewer inserted into the middle comes out clean. Leave to cool in the tin for five minutes then turn out onto a wire rack to cool completely. The cake can be frozen at this stage if you like.

While the cakes are baking, make the icing by beating the icing sugar with the butter until light and fluffy, then folding the vanilla essence into the icing. Put this to one side until you are ready to ice the cake.

Once the coffee cakes have completely cooled, spread half the icing on the bottom of one (leaving half for the top of the cake) and sandwich the two parts together. Spread the remaining icing on top. Decorate with walnuts, or anything else you prefer.

The following recipe for ever-popular ginger cake came from Mrs Slater, who is described in the introduction as a Frenchwoman, and a most excellent cook. She and her husband looked after Steve's house in London, and made all the family comfortable there.

MRS SLATER'S GINGER CAKE

¾ lb flour	*8 ozs. butter*
2 ozs. citron peel	*5 ozs. caster sugar*
3 eggs	*3 ozs. glacé ginger*
½ gill of milk	*3 ozs. glacé cherries*
1 tsp baking powder[17]	

Modern ingredients
200 g / 7 oz self-raising flour
200 g / 7 oz sugar
25 g / 1 oz candied peel
25 g / 1 oz candied ginger / chopped fresh ginger (or 1 tsp of ground ginger)
25 g / 1 oz glacé cherries
1 tsp bicarbonate of soda
55 g / 2 oz butter, plus extra for greasing
1 egg, beaten
240 ml / 9 fl oz milk

Method: Preheat the oven to 180 °C / 350 °F / gas mark 4. Grease and line a 28 cm x 18 cm / 11 in x 7 in rectangular baking tin with baking parchment.

Mix the flour, sugar, ginger, and bicarbonate of soda together in a bowl. Using your fingers, rub the butter in until the mixture resembles fine breadcrumbs, then add the candied peel, ginger, and cherries. Add the beaten egg and milk, and mix well with a wooden spoon until combined.

Pour the mixture into the prepared tin and bake in the middle of the oven for 35-40 minutes, or until golden-brown and the top is springy to the touch. Leave to cool in the tin. Once cool, cut into squares.

Notes: This makes a nice, light ginger sponge that the family would have enjoyed with afternoon tea. You may leave out the peel and/or cherries if you like, as some people may be allergic to these, but it will change the texture of the cake.

The original scone was round and flat, usually as large as a medium-sized plate, and was made first in Scotland. It was made of wheat or barley meal, and baked on a griddle (or girdle, in Scots), then cut into triangular sections for serving. Today, the large round cake would probably be called a 'bannock', and it would be the sections that would be called 'scones'.

The editors of the *Oxford English Dictionary* believe that the word might come from Middle Dutch *schoonbrot* or Middle Low German *schonbrot*, meaning 'fine bread'. This Middle Low German word is explained in the *Bremen Wörterbuch* ('Bremen Glossary') of 1771 as a sort of white loaf with two acute and two obtuse angles.[18] The first mention of the scone was in 1513, in a translation by Gavin Douglas of a line of Virgil's *Aeneid* (vii. iii. 15) which reads: 'The flour sconnis war sett in, by and by, Wyth wther mesis.' [The flour scones were put in place, by and by, with other dishes.]

When baking powder became generally available in the nineteenth century, scones began to be the oven-baked, well-leavened items we know today, although some scones, like potato scones, which my father taught me how to make, are still made on the griddle without baking powder. The secret of good scones is not to handle them too much before baking, and to make the mixture on the wet, sticky side.

My Irish granny had a very light touch with 'soda' scones, which are made with buttermilk. On a visit to see our family after we had emigrated to Canada, she brought us a bag of scones freshly baked from her cosy home at the Scottish seaside, and we agreed that no-one could make scones like granny.

Our father took away four of the scones she brought on that first trip, secretly putting them in our freezer, and the next time granny came to Canada, he told her not to bring any scones with her. When we sat down to tea on her first evening with us, the defrosted scones were produced, and granny was asked to sample one and tell us what she thought of them. If she had criticized them in any way, our father would have teased her unmercifully.

Granny, however, true to form, caught him out at his own game. In answer to his question, she cried, 'Well, if ye can mak scones like yon yerselves, ye dinna need me to mak any fer ye!' [Translation: 'Well, if you can make scones like those yourselves, you don't need me to make any for you!']

Scones

Into 2 breakfast cupfuls of flour, rub a piece of butter, the size of a walnut. Then thoroughly mix with 2 teaspoonsful of Cream of Tartar and 1 teaspoonful of carbonate of soda in milk.[19]

Ingredients:
450 g / 1 lb self-raising flour
1 tsp baking powder
2 tsps Cream of Tartar
50 g / 2 oz butter, softened, cut into pieces
225 ml / 8 fl oz milk
¼ tsp salt

Method: Pre-heat the oven to 220 ºC / 420 ºF / gas mark 7. Lightly grease two baking trays. Sift together the flour, baking powder, cream of tartar and salt into a bowl. Add the butter and rub quickly into the flour, so that it is like fine breadcrumbs.

Add the milk, a little at a time, working to a smooth dough. This is now best left to rest for 10-15 minutes before rolling.

Roll out the dough on a lightly floured work surface until 2 cm / ¾ in thick. Using a 5 cm / 2 in pastry cutter, cut the dough, using one precise movement. Do not twist the dough as you cut, as this will result in the scone not rising evenly.

Dust the scones lightly with flour, put them on the trays, and bake in the pre-heated oven for 10-12 minutes until golden-brown. Cool slightly on wire trays, and serve while still warm, if possible.

Notes: Don't over-handle the dough or it will be tough, and don't be tempted to roll it out too thinly or you won't get the lovely deep scones that are a joy to eat.

The next recipe we are going to look at is for a yeast cake with a difference – this one contains a tiny bit of baking soda along with the

yeast. I must say that before this I had only used the two ingredients together when making crumpets to be toasted around the fire at teatime, but I found that adding the baking soda changes the density of the bread slightly and gives it a lighter consistency.

The yeast cake recipe below was given by Mrs Dora Elizabeth Speirs, the wife of the local doctor. The 1911 census states that the couple had two sons and a daughter, then aged six, four and two years old.

Dr William C. Speirs of Reeth had medical qualifications from London, Switzerland and Edinburgh, and served as a doctor in the area from 1907 until 1963. Dr Speirs was well known, and stories about his exploits were often recounted in the local press. Initially he travelled to his patients on horseback, but even after he got a car, he still sometimes rode his horse, as it was a better way to reach the outlying areas of the region.

During his long career, Dr Speirs answered many calls to help patients in remote areas across the moors where the roads were frequently snowbound or flooded. On some occasions he had to spend the night away from home when called out in bad weather. It is said that he was fairly casual about payment from his patients, and sometimes accepted a chicken or some ham instead of cash.[20] His wife must also have been a resourceful person in order to make the most of their rural setting, and give her husband help if necessary.

There is an entire section devoted to Dr Speirs in the Swaledale Museum in Reeth, where some of his personal belongings, his medical bag, and instruments such as an anaesthetic mask, are on display.

When we were arranging the Edible Exhibition at which this cake was served, I asked my friend Sally Speirs, an Oxford Librarian originally from Canada (no relation to Dr Speirs), if she would like to make this cake for the event. Unfortunately she was on her Christmas holiday in Canada at the time, and couldn't make the cake, but I made it in her honour, and it was a favourite with guests.

YEAST CAKE
(MRS SPEIRS)

1 ¼ lbs. flour	4 eggs
¾ lb. sugar	½ lb. butter
¼ lb. mixed peel	1 nutmeg
1 lb. sunmaid raisins or sultanas	
1 oz. yeast	½ pint milk
½ tsp bi-carbonate of soda	

Cream butter and sugar together, add eggs, then all dry ingredients. Lastly yeast and bicarbonate of soda (mixed in a basin with warm milk). Mix with warm milk. Bake in a moderate oven.
Half quantity makes one good cake and is better kept for a fortnight.[21]

Modern ingredients (for half the quantity):
75 g / 3 oz softened butter
175 g / 6 oz sugar
1 egg (beaten)
325 g / 12 oz plain flour
50 g / 2 oz mixed peel
1 small nutmeg (grated)
225 g / 8 oz raisins or sultanas (soaked, then dried)
15 g / 1 tbsp dried yeast / 1 oz fresh yeast

75 ml / 3 fl oz milk
¼ tsp bicarbonate of soda

Method: Soak the dried fruit in warm water for about 30 minutes, then sieve and pat dry. In a small bowl, stir the yeast, bicarbonate of soda and 1 teaspoon of the sugar into the warm milk, and let it stand 10-15 minutes until foamy.

Cream the warmed butter together with the remaining sugar until it is silky, add the beaten egg, dried fruit and peel, then sift in the flour with the grated nutmeg and mix thoroughly all together with a wooden spoon.

Make a well in the centre and pour in the yeast mixture, then blend all the ingredients together, forming a soft dough. Start with a wooden spoon and finish with your hands. You can adjust it at this stage with a little more milk if the dough is too dry, or a little flour if the mixture is too runny.

Knead in the bowl or on a floured surface until the dough becomes smooth and springy. Transfer to a clean, lightly greased bowl and cover loosely with a clean, damp tea towel. Leave in a warm place to rise until roughly doubled in size – this will take 1-2 hours, depending on how warm the room is. Because of the relatively large amount of butter in the dough, the fermentation is slow and needs time and warmth to rise.

After the dough has risen, knead it again for a few seconds. Line a 2 lb loaf tin with baking parchment, or grease and flour it. Use a little more flour to help you shape the dough into a smooth oval, then put it into the tin. Cover with a clean, damp tea towel and leave to prove in a warm place for about 20 minutes, then leave in the tin for 10 minutes before turning out.

Meanwhile, heat the oven to 180 ºC / 350 ºF / gas mark 4. Bake for 20 minutes, then cool in the tin before turning out onto a wire tray to cool.

Notes: Be sure to keep the dough warm or the cake will not rise. There are no hints in the original recipe about which tins (if any) to use, but a loaf pan seems to be best.

Wild walnuts have been used in cooking since prehistoric times, and I have seen cultivated walnut trees in many southern kitchen gardens, although they are difficult to grow in a cold northern climate. The popularity of walnuts is reflected in the number of recipes written for them through the ages. The Victorians preserved and baked with them, and were very fond of pickled walnuts. The unripe fruit was gathered in June for pickling, bottled in vinegar and spices, and used during the winter.

This light and airy walnut cake gives us an idea of what the family enjoyed making with the walnuts that they might have gathered from the trees in their garden.

Walnut Cake

Beat 1 breakfast cup of caster sugar and ½ lb butter to a cream.
Sieve 2 breakfast cupfuls of flour and 1 pinch of salt, 1 teaspoonful of bicarbonate of soda, 2 teaspoonsful cream of tartar.
Chop 1 breakfast cup of walnuts finely.
Stir in the flour and ½ breakfast cup of milk to the creamed butter.
Add the walnuts and last of all stir in the stiffly white of an egg.
Bake in a moderate oven for 1 hour. If the mixture is too dry add more milk. Ice with glacé icing, decorate with half walnuts.[22]

Ingredients:
225 g / 8 oz / 1 cup butter, softened
225 g / 8 oz / 1 cup caster sugar
450 g / 1 lb / 2 cups plain flour
1 tsp baking soda
2 tsps Cream of Tartar
a pinch of salt
225 g / 8 oz / 1 cup finely chopped walnuts
100 ml / 4 fl oz / ½ cup milk
1 egg white, stiffly beaten

Ingredients for glacé icing:
250 g / 10 oz icing sugar, sifted
3 tbsps boiling water with instant coffee dissolved in it *or* 2 tbsps boiling water and 1 tbsp Camp Coffee, or other coffee and chicory essence

Method: Preheat oven to 170 ºC / 325 ºF / gas mark 3. Grease and lightly flour two 20 cm / 8 in loose-bottomed round cake tins or a 2 lb loaf tin, or line them with baking parchment so that the cake comes out easily.

Cream butter and sugar very well in a mixing bowl, until light and fluffy. Sift flour, salt, baking soda and cream of tartar into another bowl. Chop the walnuts, making sure that the pieces are no larger than the size of a pea.

Stir in the flour mixture, then the milk, into the creamed butter mixture, then add the walnuts and make sure they are well combined and distributed. Last of all, beat the white of egg into stiff peaks and fold this gently into the rest of the mixture with a metal spoon.

If using two round cake tins, spoon the cake batter mixture equally into the two baking tins and bake for 30-35 mins or until a skewer comes out clean. If using a loaf pan, keep the same temperature, and bake for about 1 hour, checking to see if the cake is done. After you have taken the cake(s) out of the oven, allow them to rest for a few minutes then remove from pans and place on a cooling rack. Allow them to cool completely before decorating.

Decorate with glacé icing. A coffee-flavoured icing goes very well with walnut cake, so you could flavour it with coffee essence such as was used in Mrs Gregory's coffee cake.

Notes: Make sure you cut the walnuts as finely as you can, because any pieces bigger than the size of a pea will sink to the bottom of the cake during baking. It is also important to cream the butter and sugar until you see the colour of the butter turn almost white. It will take around 7 minutes using the mixer for this to happen, but it is worth the extra time taken, as it produces a fluffy texture.

Sugar, flour, butter, margarine and milk were all rationed during and after the First World War, so at first I thought the recipe for 'War Cake' that I found amongst the Otterington Hall recipes must have been made in response to rationing; but then I discovered that 'War cakes' or 'Trench cakes' as they were also known, were baked and posted abroad to soldiers fighting on the front line from 1914-1918.

The government even released an official recipe for Trench cake so that the public could bake traditional cakes to be sent to the soldiers in the trenches. Some traditional ingredients were hard to come by, so in the official Trench cake recipe, more familiar cake ingredients were replaced with vinegar, milk and margarine. There were no eggs in the recipe, so vinegar was used to react with the baking soda and help the cake rise.[23]

The cakes and other provisions sent to the soldiers were very welcome, and war poets such as Ivor Gurney mentioned their arrival amid the unimaginable hardships of the front line. In his poem entitled 'Laventie', Gurney vividly conjures up for us the isolation and deprivation the soldiers must have felt:

> The letters written there, and received there,
> Books, cakes, cigarettes in a parish of famine...[24]

Bread and flour were very scarce, and by 1916 a lot of bread was being made from ground-up turnips or potatoes. The new Ministry for Food put out a leaflet with ideas for making pastry, cakes, and buns from potatoes, and even 'chocolate potato biscuits', which were actually made from a recipe at Blaenclydach Boys' School in Glamorgan.[25]

The recipe for 'War Cake' (below) was contributed by Mrs Williams, who was the wife of Sir Penry Williams, the local MP. They had married in 1890, and their home was Pinchinthorpe Hall, which took its name from the Norman family of Pinchun who first held land there in the twelfth century.

Sir Penry had a successful political career, representing Middlesbrough East as a Liberal Member of Parliament from 1918-1924, and the family entertained many guests, including the Prime Minister, Lloyd George, who stayed in their home on various occasions. Mrs Williams backed many charitable causes, and probably would have encouraged local women to bake War cakes for the soldiers that they knew.

WAR CAKE
(MRS WILLIAMS)

1 lb. flour	*½ lb. currants*
½ lb. brown sugar	*½ lb. sultanas or stoned raisins*
3 ozs. butter	*3 ozs. lard*

2 ozs. candied peel	*A gill of milk**
½ teaspoonful vinegar	*2 small teaspoonsful grated nutmeg*
Pinch of salt	*1 teaspoonful bi-carbonate of soda*

Put flour, salt and spice into a dry bowl. Rub the lard in, and butter, until fine. Add the fruit, etc. and mix well. Mix the soda with the milk to which add the vinegar. Stir into the dry ingredients sufficient to make a stiff mixture. Pour into a well greased tin and bake for about 2 hours.

It is better made into two cakes and it requires well baking.[26]

* A gill=approximately 100 ml / 4 fl oz / ½ cup.

Notes: The instructions above are easy to follow, and do not need much further explanation. These cakes may be made in two 20cm / 8 in round cake tins (one tin for half the mixture) and should be baked at 180 °C / 350 °F / gas mark 4.

Shrewsbury cakes (or biscuits) are a type of shortbread, and have a long and varied history. They were originally made in Shrewsbury in Shropshire, giving them their name. We know that they date from at least the seventeenth century, because there were several early literary references to them, including the expression 'as short as a Shrewsbury cake', used by playwright William Congreve in his play *The Way of the World*, published in 1700. The earliest recorded recipe for these biscuits seems to be one in *The Compleat Cook*, printed in 1658 and attributed to someone with the initials 'W.M.' This earliest recipe uses rosewater and ginger to flavour the biscuits, but in later recipes, nutmeg, cinnamon and sometimes caraway seeds were used to spice them.

The recipe for Shrewsbury cakes in the *Otterington Hall Recipe Book* is a plain and simple unattributed one, which gives only minimal cooking directions. The recipe mentions 'ratafia', and this is a fruit brandy. In *A Word-Book of Wine*, written in 1959, Walter James explains: '*Ratafias* were infusions of fruit or herbs in brandy, made by housewives in happier days when brandy was cheap.'[27]

Shrewsbury Cakes

¾ lb. flour	*¼ lb. butter*
6 ozs. sugar	*2 eggs*
2 teaspoonsful baking powder	*A few drops of ratafia*

Sprinkle chopped almonds over cake.[28]

Modern ingredients for half of the original recipe (makes 24 biscuits):
175 g / 6 oz plain flour
50 g / 2 oz cold butter
75 g / 3 oz caster sugar
1 egg
1 tsp brandy
1 tsp baking powder
50 g / 2 oz chopped almonds for sprinkling (optional)

Method: Sieve the baking powder and flour into a bowl, and rub the butter into the flour mixture using your fingertips until it is like fine breadcrumbs. Add the rest of the ingredients and mix all together with your hands, until everything is incorporated. Shape the dough into a flattened disc and wrap it in cling film or a plastic bag and put it in the fridge for 30 minutes.

Sprinkle the work surface with flour and roll the dough until it is about 6 mm / ¼ in thick. Make the biscuits any shape you like and place regularly on lightly greased or parchment-covered baking sheets. Sprinkle with the chopped almonds at this stage if you wish.

Put in the centre of a preheated oven at 170 ºC / 325 ºF / gas mark 3, and bake in the centre of the oven for 8-10 minutes until the biscuits are a light golden brown. These biscuits are delicate, so leave them on the trays to cool for five minutes and then place them carefully onto wire racks and cover with a cloth until they are cool.

If the biscuits have not been covered in chopped almonds, they could be iced with glacé icing at this stage, or two could be sandwiched together with jam for serving.

The recipe which finishes our selection of country house confections comes from 'Woodlands' in West Hartlepool, the home of another of Mary and Steve's great aunts, Mrs Christopher Brown. Built in 1879, Woodlands was very close to Tunstall Grange, where Mary and Steve used to live as children. They describe it in their preface as 'a house with all the solid comfort and good management of the Edwardian era'.

The recipe chosen from Woodlands is one for German Biscuits. Do you remember Eliza Acton's recipe for *Appel Krapfen* in the preceding chapter? In it, she wrote: '...the Germans add a rather high flavouring of cinnamon, which is a very favourite spice with them'. The addition of cinnamon to the recipe for the biscuits below might be the reason for their name.

German Biscuits
(Woodlands)

½ lb. butter   *½ lb. flour*
½ lb. sugar   *1 egg*
1 teaspoonful cinnamon

Mix as pastry. Roll out. Cut into small rounds. When baked, join together with a little jam. Ice and decorate.[29]

Method: Cream the butter and sugar together until light and fluffy, and then break the egg into the bowl and mix it all together with a wooden spoon.

Mix in the sieved flour and cinnamon, and knead until it all comes together. Put the dough into the refrigerator for about an hour to firm up the butter and help to prevent the biscuits spreading while they are baking.

Roll out the dough on a floured work surface to about 6 mm / ¼ in thick. Cut into small rounds and place on a lined baking sheet. It will make 12-15 biscuits.

Bake in a preheated oven at 170 ºC / 325 ºF / gas mark 3 for about 10 minutes. Leave to cool briefly on the trays before transferring to a wire rack.

Sandwich two of the biscuits together using a teaspoonful of jam (piquant flavours like raspberry or blackcurrant are best to contrast with the sweet icing) and then cover the top biscuit with icing. To make the glacé icing, mix 150g / 5 oz icing sugar with 25 ml / 1 ½ tablespoons of boiling water. Top each biscuit with half a glacé cherry or other decoration while the icing is still wet.

Notes: This is another biscuit that my mother made for us, and my task as a three-year-old was to add the jaunty cherry on top of each one, accompanied by laughs, hugs, and smears of icing on hands and aprons – a perfect introduction to the joys of baking!

The recipes for the cakes and biscuits given in this last cookbook may seem very different from the 'messes' and elaborate 'subtleties' of the fourteenth and fifteenth centuries, but when we look more closely, the standard elements from that bygone era, such as flour, eggs, dairy products and spices, have stood the test of time and are still used today. With the help of experimentation in new techniques and inventions, these ancient ingredients have been combined together in fresh ways, culminating in confections like elegant meringues and airy sponge cakes which would have seemed miraculous to our predecessors.

When I planned to include some of the sweet dishes from the *Otterington Hall Recipe Book* as part of an alumni event so long ago, I had no idea that this first celebration would become a lasting tradition at Oriel College. Those of us who produced items for the Edible Exhibitions learned by trial and error, and were delighted and disappointed in turn by our efforts, echoing the experience of cooks through the ages, who have taught us so much by their writings.

I hope that you will be able to recreate many of the unusual sweet dishes presented within these pages, and will choose some favourites of your own to enjoy.

Happy baking!

ACKNOWLEDGEMENTS

Sweet Slices of History was conjured up in only a few short months, but it owes its life to sixteen years of research and experience, and its roots extend much farther back than that; so it is no wonder that I owe a huge number of people an enormous debt of gratitude.

Speaking of roots, I have to start with Granny Rae – the only grandmother I was privileged to know – but what a generous heart she had! She and my parents, by their example, taught my brother and myself that everything you provide should be given out of love and care for others.

This book is based on the Edible Exhibitions which took place at Oriel College, Oxford, from 2002-2017. The name of the event was thought up by my friend Caroline Weston, and I adopted it immediately!

I am extremely grateful to successive Provosts, Fellow Librarians, and other Fellows of Oriel for allowing me to host the Edible Exhibitions in the beautiful Senior Common Room; grateful too to the many people who made decorative dishes to present at those feasts, and to everyone who attended. Many thanks are due to Oriel's Head Chef, Steve Morris, the sous-chefs, and SCR staff, who did everything in their power to make the events successful. I also want to thank Rupert and Dave for crafting the elegant triangular R&D recipe holders.

I could not have done the necessary research without my colleagues in libraries and archives. I particularly want to thank Alexander Devine of Corpus Christi College, Cambridge; Rob Petre of Oriel College, Oxford; Julian Reid and Joanna Snelling of Corpus Christi College, Oxford, and Christopher Skelton-Foord of New College, Oxford.

I have also benefited from the generosity of the Blencowe family, Peter Brears, Helen M Clifford, the Furness family, The Ivor Gurney Trust, and Christina Stapley, and am deeply indebted to all of these people.

As for the book itself, I thank Catheryn Kilgarriff most sincerely for taking a chance on me as an untried author, and for considering this book worthy of publication; and I appreciate Brendan King's careful editing and helpful comments about the script. Heartfelt thanks to Tim Kirtley for his lively and sensitive drawings, which capture the essence of the Edible Exhibitions so beautifully.

Many photographers have had a part in making up the book, and I thank David Archer, Merridee Bailey, Heather M Bush, Linda Bush Cannon, Colin Dunn, David Stumpp, and Christian Szurko for their fine photography. Special thanks go to Elizabeth Adams and Pamela Kat Johnson for dropping everything at short notice to bake their dishes before photographing them artistically – how's that for friendship?

ACKNOWLEDGEMENTS

Marilyn Yurdan and Peter Davidson suggested that I seek a publisher, and helped me take the project forward. David Maskell furnished me with the name of the book by a chance remark long ago, and Merridee Bailey read the first chapter and suggested improvements. The coffee shop trio of Wilma, Isabel, and Peter supported me, and members of the Cod Squad picked me up and dusted me off at various times. Bronac shared her knowledge of the All Souls accounts, and found a healthy borage plant in time for me to make borage tarts. My friends at St Stephen's House have welcomed me, and enjoyed my cakes!

I'm grateful for kind friends like Pauline and Roberta taking me out for coffee, for meals, to the countryside, on picnics, and to the theatre and cinema. Even our neighbour, Tony, has helped, by tending our front lawn.

My brother Peter and his family, and my son John and his wife Rosalind have never failed to encourage me, but most of all, I want to thank my husband Christian for all his help. Giving me hugs at night and endless cups of coffee in the mornings, he has lent endless support in the best and the worst of times, and framed my days with love.

Marjory M Szurko,
Abingdon, 2018.

PICTURE CREDITS

Drawings on pages 9, 69, 101, 130 and 185 by Tim Kirtley.

Photographs on pages 2, 53, 87 and 201 by Pamela Kat Johnson.

Photographs on pages 11, 12, 29, 40, 49, 59, 81, 83, 106, 121, 123, 179 and 183 by Christian Szurko.

Photographs on pages 17, 18, 75 and 76 by Linda Bush Cannon.

Photographs on pages 25 and 26 by Elizabeth Adams.

Photograph on page 62 by Colin Dunn/Scriptura (reproduced by permission of the President and Fellows of Corpus Christi College, Oxford).

Photograph on page 67 by Catheryn Kilgarriff.

Photographs on pages 94, 99, 146 and 152 by David Stumpp.

Photograph on page 102 by David Archer.

Illustrations on page 129 reproduced by kind permission of the Provost, Fellows and Scholars of Oriel College, Oxford.

Photographs on pages 154, 158, 163 and 186 by Merridee Bailey.

NOTES

Introduction
1 Furness, Stephen & Mary (eds). *Otterington Hall Recipe Book* (Printed for Mary and Stephen Furness by North End Press, Northallerton, n.d. [1969]).
2 Hieatt, Constance B. & Sharon Butler (eds). *Curye on Inglysch: English Culinary Manuscripts of the Fourteenth Century (including The Forme of Cury)*, (Oxford: Published for the Early English Text Society by Oxford University Press, 1985).
3 Austin, Thomas (ed.). *Two Fifteenth-Century Cookery-Books* (Oxford: Published for the Early English Text Society by the Oxford University Press, 1964).

Chapter One
1 Aresty, Esther B. *The Delectable Past* (London: George Allen & Unwin, 1965), p. 18.
2 Aresty, p. 20.
3 Austin, op.cit., pp. 67-68.
4 Austin, pp. 57-58.
5 Austin, p.146.
6 Hieatt, op. cit., p. 3.
7 Hieatt, pp. 204-05.
8 Hieatt, p. 113.
9 Hieatt, p. 144.
10 Hieatt, p. 206.
11 Sass, Lorna. *To the King's Taste: Richard II's Book of Feasts and Recipes Adapted for Modern Cooking* (London: John Murray, 1976), p. 85.
12 Hieatt, p. 132.
13 Sass, p. 48.
14 Hieatt, p. 137.
15 Hieatt, p.138.
16 Hieatt, pp. 191-2.
17 Hieatt, p. 154.
18 Purseglove, John William. *Spices,* Vol.1. (London: Longman, 1981).
19 Hieatt, p. 142.
20 Friedman, John Block. *Northern English Books, Owners, and Makers in the Late Middle Ages* (New York: Syracuse University Press, 1995), p.86.
21 Hieatt, p. 152.
22 Hieatt, p. 153.

Chapter Two
1 *ESTC (English Short Title Catalogue)* 3297.
2 Redstone, Vincent B. (ed.). *The Household Book of Dame Alice de Bryene, of Acton Hall, Suffolk, Sept. 1412 – Sept. 1413*. With appendices. Ttranslated by Miss M.K. Dale. Suffolk Institute of Archaeology and Natural History (Ipswich: Harrison, 1931), pp. 103-04.
3 The word 'frail' in this context derives from Old French *frael* meaning 'rush basket' from classical Latin *flagellum*, rather than from the Latin *fragilis* meaning 'fragile'.
4 Redstone, p. 121.

5   'Short Notices', *The English Historical Review*, Vol. 47, No. 188 (Oct. 1932), pp. 703-4.
6   Milham, Mary Ella (tr.). *Platina, On Right Pleasure and Good Health: A Critical Edition and Translation of De honesta voluptate et valetudine* (Tempe, Arizona: Medieval and Renaissance Texts and Studies, 1988), Book 1, pp. 13-14.
7   Austin, p. 52.
8   Austin, pp. 7-8.
9   Austin, p. 46.
10 Pipe Roll Society, *The Great Roll of the Pipe for the Seventeenth Year of the Reign of King Henry the Second A.D. 1170-1,* (London: The Pipe Roll Society, 1893), p.12.
11 Austin, pp 106-7.
12 Austin, p. 35.
13 Austin, p. 51.
14 Corpus Christi College, Oxford MS 291 (18), 15r.
15 Austin, p. 34.
16 Austin, p. 35.
17 Austin, p. 97.
18 Austin, p. 97.
19 Austin, p. 68.

Chapter Three
1   Oriel College Archives, 1596 inventory, ETC A8/12.
2   Jones, E. Alfred. *Catalogue of the Plate of Oriel College, Oxford*, 2nd issue (London: Oxford University Press, 1944), p. 73.
3   Jones, p. 18.
4   Clifford, Helen M. *A Treasured Inheritance: 600 Years of Oxford College Silver* (Oxford: Ashmolean Museum, 2004), pp. 66-69.
5   Furnivall, Frederick J. *Early English Meals and Manners* (London: Early English Text Society, 1868), p. 22.
6   von Drachenfels, Suzanne. *The Art of the Table: A Complete Guide to Table Setting, Table Manners and Tableware* (New York, Simon & Schuster, 2000), pp. 90-91.
7   'Thynne, William', Sidney Lee, revised by A.S.G. Edwards, *Oxford Dictionary of National Biography*, <https://doi.org/10.1093/ref:odnb/27426>.
8   Lindberg, D.C. *The Beginnings of Western Science: the European Scientific Tradition in Philosophical, Religious, and Institutional Context, 600 B.C. to A.D. 1450* (Chicago: University of Chicago Press, 2007).
9   Gerard, John. *The Herball or Generall Historie of Plantes* (London, 1597), pp. 151-7.
10 Furnivall, Frederick J. & M.T. Culley (eds). *Caxton's Eneydos 1490* (London: Early English Text Society by the Oxford University Press, 1890), pp. 2-3.
11 Baddeley, Susan & Anja Voeste. *Orthographies in Early Modern Europe* (Berlin: De Gruyter Mouton, 2012), p. 148.
12 Dawson, Thomas. *The Good Huswifes Handmaide for the Kitchin* (London, 1594), f.51r and 51v.
13 Ahmed, Anne (ed.). *A Proper Newe Booke of Cokerye: Margaret Parker's Cookery Book* (Cambridge: Corpus Christi College, 2002), pp. 1-11 (used by permission of The Parker Library, Corpus Christi College, Cambridge).
14 Gerard, pp. 796-98.
15 *A Proper Newe Booke of Cokerye*, [1557] f. 187r (used by permission of The Parker Library, Corpus Christi College, Cambridge).
16 Dawson, *The Good Huswifes Handmaide*, f.29r. and 29v.

17 Dawson, *The Good Huswifes Handmaide,* f.43v. and 44r.
18 Dawson, *The Good Huswifes Handmaide,* f.31v.
19 Gerard, pp. 926-28.
20 Dawson, *The Good Huswifes Handmaide,* f.32r. and 32v.
21 Dawson, *The Good Huswifes Handmaide,* f.31r. and 31v.
22 Dawson, *The Good Huswifes Handmaide,* f.17r.
23 Dawson, *The Good Huswifes Handmaide,* f.52r.
24 'Tragacanth', Colony Gums <htpp:www.colonygums.com/tragacanth>.
25 Dawson, Thomas. *The Second Part of the Good huswifes Jewell* (London, 1597), p. 39.
26 [A.W.]. *A Book of Cookrye: Very Necessary for All Such as Delight Therin* (London: Edward Allde, 1591).
27 Brears, Peter. *All the King's Cooks: the Tudor Kitchens of King Henry VIII at Hampton Court Palace* (London: Souvenir Press, 2011), pp. 177-78. (Used by kind permission of the author.)
28 Durning, Louise (ed.). *Queen Elizabeth's Book of Oxford* (Oxford: Bodleian Library, 2006).

Chapter Four
1 Floyd, Janet & Laurel Forster (eds.). *The Recipe Reader: Narratives, Contexts, Traditions* (Aldershot: Ashgate, 2003), p.6.
2 Spiller, Elizabeth. *Science, Reading and Renaissance Literature: The Art of Making Knowledge, 1580-1670* (Cambridge: Cambridge University Press, 2004), p. 10.
3 Floyd, p. 6.
4 [Plat, Sir Hugh]. *A Closet for Ladies and Gentlewomen* (London: 1608), p. 33.
5 Markham, Gervase. *The English Housewife (1615)*, ed. Michael R Best (Montreal: McGill-Queen's University Press, 1994), Recipe 172, p. 115.
6 *Oxford English Dictionary online* (accessed 23 May 2018).
7 Driver, Christopher (ed.). *John Evelyn, Cook: the Manuscript Receipt Book of John Evelyn* (Devon, Prospect Books, 1997), Receipt No. 80.
8 Driver, Receipt No. 111.
9 May, Robert. *The Accomplist Cook or the Art and Mystery of Cooking* (London, 1660), p. 262.
10 *Oxford English Dictionary online* (accessed 1 June 2018).
11 May, p. 271
12 Woolley, Hannah. *The Gentlewoman's Companion or, a Guide to the Female Sex*, with an introduction by Caterina Albano (London, Prospect Books, 2001), p. 7-9.
13 Woolley, *The Gentlewoman's Companion*, pp. 144-45
14 Woolley, Hannah. *The Cooks Guide: Or, Rare Receipts for Cookery* (London, 1664), p. 4.
15 Woolley, Hannah. *The Accomplish'd Lady's Delight in Preserving, Physick, Beautifying, and Cookery,* Second edition enlarged (London: B. Harris, 1677), p. 294.
16 *Oxford English Dictionary online* (accessed 14 May 2018).
17 Stapley, Christina (ed.). *The Receipt Book of Lady Anne Blencowe* (Basingstoke: Heartsease Books, 2004), p. 1.
18 Saintsbury, George (ed.). *The Receipt Book of Mrs Ann Blencowe A.D.1694* (London: Chapman, 1925), p. 6.
19 Saintsbury, p. 7.
20 *Oxford English Dictionary.*
21 Davidson, Alan (ed.). *The Oxford Companion to Food* (Oxford: Oxford University Press, 1999), p. 178.
22 'Discovering Chocolate: The Great Chocolate Discovery', Cadbury <https://www.cadbury.com.au/about-chocolate/discovering-chocolate.aspx>.

23 Stapley, pp. 33-34 (with permission).

24 Saintsbury, p. 35.

25 Driver, Receipt No. 206.

26 Sandford, Francis. *The History and Coronation of James II* (London, 1687).

Chapter Five

1 'White, Gilbert (1720-1793)', by Paul Foster, *Oxford Dictionary of National Biography* <https://doi.org/10.1093/ref:odnb/29243>.

2 'Brummell, George Bryan [known as Beau Brummell] (1778-1840)', by Philip Carter, *Oxford Dictionary of National Biography* <https://doi.org/10.1093/ref:odnb/3771>.

3 [Ayres, Ralph] *A Little Book of Recipes of New College Two Hundred Years Ago*, edited by L.G. Wickham Legg (Oxford: Oxford University Press, 1922), p. 2.

4 New College Library, Oxford, NCA 962, f.20r.

5 Mintz, Sidney W. *Sweetness and Power: The Place of Sugar in Modern History* (New York: Viking Penguin, 1985), pp. 66-7.

6 [Kettilby, Mary]. *A Collection of Above Three Hundred Receipts in Cookery, Physick and Surgery* (London, 1714), Preface [p. 9].

7 Smith, Eliza. *The Compleat Housewife* (London, 1729), Preface [p. 5].

8 Glasse, Hannah. *The Art of Cookery, Made Plain and Easy*, 4th edition (London, 1751), p. i.

9 'Glasse [née Allgood], Hannah', by A. H. T. Robb-Smith, *Oxford Dictionary of National Biography* < https://doi.org/10.1093/ref:odnb/10804>.

10 Glasse, p. 274.

11 Glasse, p. 277.

12 Smith, Preface [p. 5].

13 Smith, Preface [p. 6].

14 Glasse, p. iii.

15 Raffald, Elizabeth. *The Experienced English Housekeeper* (London, 1769), Title page.

16 'Raffald [née Whitaker] Elizabeth' Nancy Cox, *Oxford Dictionary of National Biography* < https://doi.org/10.1093/ref:odnb/23008>.

17 Raffald, p. 245.

18 Raffald, pp. 168-9.

19 'Potential Toxic Levels of Cyanide in Almonds (*Prunus amygdalus*), Apricot Kernels (*Prunus armeniaca*), and Almond Syrup', by Nadia Chaouali, et al. in *ISRN Toxicology*, 19 September 2013. <https://www.hindawi.com/journals/isrn/2013/610648/>.

20 Raffald, p. 170.

21 Spurling, Hilary. *Elinor Fettiplace's Receipt Book* (London: Viking Salamander, 1986).

22 Raffald, pp. 254-5.

23 Clermont, Bernard. *The Professed Cook; or, the Modern Art of Cookery, Pastry, & Confectionary, made Plain and Easy* (London, 3rd ed., 1776). Title page.

24 Feirstein, Sanna. *Naming New York: Manhattan Places and How They Got Their Names* (New York: New York University Press, 2001), p. 89.

25 'Bertie, Willoughby, fourth earl of Abingdon (1740-1799)' by William C. Lowe, *Oxford Dictionary of National Biography* <https://doi.org/10.1093/ref:odnb/2280>.

26 Clermont, p. 393.

27 Clermont, pp. 419-20.

28 Ayto, John (ed.). *An A-Z of Food and Drink* (Oxford: Oxford University Press, 2002).

29 *The Poor Print* (Oriel College Newspaper) 4 March 2016.

30 Clermont, p. 429.

31 Clermont, pp. 422-23.

32 Clermont, p. 432.

Chapter Six

1   Mollard, John. *The Art of Cookery Made Easy and Refined*. New edition (London: Whittaker, 1836), p. iv.

2   Mollard, p. 244.

3   Davidson, Alan, p. 748.

4   'Springerle, Germany 14th Century', Sweet Tooth Design <https://www.sweetoothdesign.com/cookie-springerle>.

5   Goldstein, Darra (ed.). *The Oxford Companion to Sugar and Sweets* (Oxford: Oxford University Press, 2015) p. 473.

6   'Block Gingerbread', Food History Jottings, a blog by Ivan Day <http://foodhistorjottings.blogspot.com/2013/07/block-gingerbread.html>.

7   Read, George. *The Complete Biscuit and Gingerbread Baker's Assistant* (London: Dean & Son, 1854), p. 83-84.

8   Hone, William (ed.). *The Every-day Book, or Everlasting Calendar of Popular Amusements* (London: Hunt & Clarke, 1826), p. 576.

9   Mollard, p. 247.

10 Mollard, pp. 237-8

11 Mollard, p. 289.

12 Mollard, p. 289.

13 Acton, Eliza. *Modern Cookery in all its Branches* (London: Longman, 1845), p. ix-x.

14 Acton, *Modern Cookery in all its Branches*, p. vii.

15 Acton, *Modern Cookery in all its Branches*, p. x.

16 'Acton, Eliza (1799-1859)', by Elizabeth Ray, *Oxford Dictionary of National Biography* <https://doi.org/10.1093/ref:odnb/73>.

17 Acton, *Modern cookery in all its Branches*, p.360.

18 'Alfred Bird: Egg-free custard inventor and chemist', *Birmingham Mail*, <https://www.birminghammail.co.uk/incoming/alfred-bird-egg-free-custard-inventor-8040314> Retrieved 25 February 2018.

19 Moore, John T. (ed.). *Chemistry Made Simple* (New York: Broadway Books, 2005), p. 190.

20 Shipman, Matt. 'The difference between baking soda and baking powder' in *NC State News* (Raleigh, North Carolina, USA: NC State University, May 21, 2014).

21 Matz, Samuel A. *Bakery Technology and Engineering* (New York: Springer, 1992), p. 54.

22 Beeton, Isabella. *Mrs Beeton's Book of Household Management* (London: S Beeton, 1861), p. 856.

23 Read, p. 83.

24 Acton, *Modern Cookery in all its Branches*, p. 517.

25 Zapp, Karl-Heinz. 'Ammonium Compounds' in *Ullmann's Encyclopedia of Industrial Chemistry* (Weinheim: Wiley-VCH, 2012).

26 Acton, Eliza. *Modern Cookery for Private Families* (London: Quadrille, 2011), p. 373.

27 'Beeton [née Mayson], Isabella Mary (1836-1865)' *Oxford Dictionary of National Biography* <https://doi.org/10.1093/ref:odnb/37172>.

28 Beeton, Part IX, Paragraph 1451.

29 Beeton, Part IX, Paragraph 1740.

30 Mokyr, Joel (ed.). *The Oxford Encyclopedia of Economic History*, Vol. 3 (New York: Oxford University Press, 2003), p. 343.

31 'Tea-Table Talk: a woman's letter to women', *Cardiff Times and South Wales Weekly News*, 30

October 1891 <https://blog.britishnewspaperarchive.co.uk/2017/03/23/cookery-corner-cakes/>.

32 'Soyer, Alexis Benoît (1810–1858)', by Elizabeth Ray, *Oxford Dictionary of National Biography* (Oxford: OUP, 2004) <https://doi.org/10.1093/ref:odnb/26076>.

33 Soyer, Alexis. *A Shilling Cookery for the People* (London: Routledge, 1854), Recipe 388A, p. 143.

34 Soyer, Alexis. *The Gastronomic Regenerator: A Simplified and Entirely New System of Cookery* (Cambridge: Cambridge University Press, originally published 1846, digitally printed version 2013), Recipe 1327, pp. 569-70.

Chapter Seven

1 Furness, op. cit.

2 'Stephen Furness', The Peerage <http://www.thepeerage.com/p41556.htm#i415559>.

3 Oxford English Dictionary (Oxford: Oxford University Press).

4 Ayto, op. cit.

5 Furness, p. 17.

6 Bryan, Annette. *Yesterday* (Oxford: Oxford University Press, 1973), p. v.

7 Bryan, p. 2.

8 Furness, p. 19.

9 Furness, p. 20.

10 'Furness, Christopher, first Baron Furness (1852-1912)', Gordon Boyce, *Oxford Dictionary of National Biography* <https://doi.org/10.1093/ref:odnb/33295>.

11 'Grantley Hall History, Part Two: The Furness Family', Grantley Hall <https://www.grantleyhall.co.uk/news/grantley-hall-history,-part-two--the-furness-family/56-6/>.

12 'Japanese Garden at Grantley Hall', Historic England <https://historicengland.org.uk/listing/the-list/list-entry/1442593>.

13 'Rum' in *Encyclopaedia Britannica*.

14 Furness, p. 21. Metric measurements for the ingredients have been added.

15 'Chicory on Phillip Island', Australian Food History Timeline <https://australianfoodtimeline.com.au/1870-chicory-on-phillip-island/>.

16 Furness, p. 23.

17 Furness, p. 25.

18 *Oxford English Dictionary* (Oxford: Oxford University Press).

19 Furness, p. 26.

20 'A Look at Health and Sickness in Upper Swaledale and Arkengarthdale (2017)', by Jocelyn M. Campbell <https://swaag.org/pdf/DalesHealth-JocelynCampbell.pdf>.

21 Furness, p. 27.

22 Furness, p. 28.

23 'How to bake a First World War Trench cake', *The Telegraph*, 18 August 2018 < https://www.telegraph.co.uk/history/world-war-one/10905975/How-to-bake-a-First-World-War-trench-cake.html>.

24 Gurney, Ivor. *Collected Poems of Ivor Gurney*, edited by P. J. Kavanagh (Oxford: Oxford University Press, 1982), pp. 77–78. (By kind permission of Ivor Gurney Trust.)

25 'Blaenclydach Boys and the Chocolate Potato Biscuits', by Tony Peters, Glamorgan Archives <https://glamarchives.wordpress.com/2015/05/06/blaenclydach-boys-and-the-chocolate-potato-biscuits/>.

26 Furness, p. 29.

27 'Ratafias'. James, Walter. *A Word-Book of Wine* (London: Phoenix, 1959).

28 Furness, p. 30.

29 Furness, p. 32.

BIBLIOGRAPHY

Acton, Eliza. *Modern Cookery for Private Families* (London: Quadrille, 2011).

Acton, Eliza. *Modern Cookery in all its Branches* (London: Longman, 1845).

Ahmed, Anne (ed.), *A Proper Newe Booke of Cokerye: Margaret Parker's Cookery Book* (Cambridge: Corpus Christi College, 2002).

Aresty, Esther B. *The Delectable Past* (London: George Allen & Unwin, 1965).

Austin, Thomas (ed.). *Two Fifteenth-Century Cookery-Books* (Oxford: Published for the Early English Text Society by the Oxford University Press, 1964).

[A.W.], *A Book of Cookrye: Very Necessary for All Such as Delight Therin* (London: Edward Allde, 1591).

Aylmer, Ursula (ed.). *Oxford Food: An Anthology* (Oxford: Ashmolean, 1995).

[Ayres, Ralph] *A Little Book of Recipes of New College Two Hundred Years Ago*, edited by L.G. Wickham Legg (Oxford: Oxford University Press, 1922).

Ayto, John (ed.). *An A-Z of Food and Drink* (Oxford: Oxford University Press, 2002).

Baddeley, Susan & Anja Voeste. *Orthographies in Early Modern Europe* (Berlin: De Gruyter Mouton, 2012).

Beeton, Isabella. *Mrs Beeton's Book of Household Management* (London: S Beeton, 1861).

Brears, Peter. *All the King's Cooks: the Tudor Kitchens of King Henry VIII at Hampton Court Palace* (London: Souvenir Press, 2011).

Bryan, Annette. *Yesterday* (Oxford: Oxford University Press, 1973).

Clermont, Bernard. *The Professed Cook; or, the Modern Art of Cookery, Pastry, & Confectionary, made Plain and Easy* (London, 3rd edition, 1776).

Clifford, Helen M. *A Treasured Inheritance: 600 Years of Oxford College Silver* (Oxford: Ashmolean Museum, 2004).

Davidson, Alan (ed.). *The Oxford Companion to Food* (Oxford: Oxford University Press, 1999).

Dawson, Thomas. *The Good Huswifes Handmaide for the Kitchin* (London, 1594).

Dawson, Thomas. *The Second Part of the Good huswifes Jewell* (London, 1597).

Driver, Christopher (ed.). *John Evelyn, Cook: the Manuscript Receipt Book of John Evelyn* (Devon, Prospect Books, 1997).

Durning, Louise (ed.). *Queen Elizabeth's Book of Oxford* (Oxford: Bodleian Library, 2006).

Feirstein, Sanna. *Naming New York: Manhattan Places and How They Got Their Names* (New York: New York University Press, 2001).

Floyd, Janet & Laurel Forster (eds.). *The Recipe Reader: Narratives, Contexts, Traditions* (Aldershot: Ashgate, 2003).

Friedman, John Block. *Northern English Books, Owners, and Makers in the Late Middle Ages* (New York: Syracuse University Press, 1995).

Furness, Stephen & Mary (eds). *Otterington Hall Recipe Book* (Printed for Mary and Stephen Furness by North End Press, Northallerton, n.d. [1969]).

Furnivall, Frederick J. *Early English Meals and Manners* (London: Early English Text Society, 1868).

Furnivall, Frederick J. & M.T. Culley (eds). *Caxton's Eneydos 1490* (London: Early English Text Society by the Oxford University Press, 1890).

BIBLIOGRAPHY

Gerard, John. *The Herball or Generall Historie of Plantes* (London, 1597).

Glasse, Hannah. *The Art of Cookery, Made Plain and Easy*, 4th edition (London, 1751).

Goldstein, Darra (ed.). *The Oxford Companion to Sugar and Sweets* (Oxford: Oxford University Press, 2015).

Gurney, Ivor. *Collected Poems of Ivor Gurney*, edited by P. J. Kavanagh (Oxford: Oxford University Press, 1982).

Hieatt, Constance B. & Sharon Butler (eds). *Curye on Inglysch: English Culinary Manuscripts of the Fourteenth Century (including The Forme of Cury)*, (Oxford: Published for the Early English Text Society by Oxford University Press, 1985).

Hone, William (ed.). *The Every-Day Book, or Everlasting Calendar of Popular Amusements* (London: Hunt & Clarke, 1826).

James, Walter. *A Word-Book of Wine* (London: Phoenix, 1959).

Jones, E. Alfred. *Catalogue of the Plate of Oriel College, Oxford*, 2nd issue (London: Oxford University Press, 1944).

[Kettilby, Mary]. *A Collection of Above Three Hundred Receipts in Cookery, Physick and Surgery* (London, 1714).

Lindberg, D.C. *The Beginnings of Western Science: the European Scientific Tradition in Philosophical, Religious, and Institutional Context, 600 B.C. to A.D. 1450* (Chicago: University of Chicago Press, 2007).

Markham, Gervase. *The English Housewife (1615)*, edited by Michael R Best (Montreal: McGill-Queen's University Press, 1994).

Matz, Samuel A. *Bakery Technology and Engineering* (New York: Springer, 1992).

May, Robert. *The Accomplisht Cook or the Art and Mystery of Cooking* (London: Nathaniel Brooke 1660).

Milham, Mary Ella (tr.). *Platina, On Right Pleasure and Good Health: A Critical Edition and Translation of De honesta voluptate et valetudine* (Tempe, Arizona: Medieval and Renaissance Texts and Studies, 1988).

Mintz, Sidney W. *Sweetness and Power: The Place of Sugar in Modern History* (New York: Viking Penguin, 1985).

Mokyr, Joel (ed.). *The Oxford Encyclopedia of Economic History*, Vol. 3 (New York: Oxford University Press, 2003).

Mollard, John. *The Art of Cookery Made Easy and Refined* (London: Whittaker, 1836).

Moore, John T. (ed.). *Chemistry Made Simple* (New York: Broadway Books, 2005).

Pipe Roll Society, *The Great Roll of the Pipe for the Seventeenth Year of the Reign of King Henry the Second A.D. 1170-1* (London: The Pipe Roll Society, 1893).

Plat, Sir Hugh. *Delightes for Ladies to Adorn their Persons, Tables, Closets, and Distillatories: with Beauties, Banquets, Perfumes and Waters* (London: Peter Short, c. 1602).

[Plat, Sir Hugh]. *A Closet for Ladies and Gentlewomen* (London: 1608).

Purseglove, John William. *Spices*, Vol.1. (London: Longman, 1981).

Pynson, Richard. *This is the Boke of Cokery* (London: Richard Pynson, 1500).

Raffald, Elizabeth. *The Experienced English Housekeeper* (London, 1769).

Read, George. *The Complete Biscuit and Gingerbread Baker's Assistant* (London: Dean & Son, 1854).

Redstone, Vincent B. (ed.). *The Household Book of Dame Alice de Bryene, of Acton Hall, Suffolk, Sept. 1412 – Sept. 1413*. With appendices. Translated by Miss M.K. Dale. Suffolk Institute of Archaeology and Natural History (Ipswich: Harrison, 1931).

BIBLIOGRAPHY

Saintsbury, George (ed.). *The Receipt Book of Mrs Ann Blencowe A.D.1694* (London: Chapman, 1925).

Sandford, Francis. *The History and Coronation of James II* (London, 1687).

Sass, Lorna. *To the King's Taste: Richard II's Book of Feasts and Recipes Adapted for Modern Cooking* (London: John Murray, 1976).

Shipman, Matt. 'The difference between baking soda and baking powder' in *NC State News* (Raleigh, North Carolina, USA: NC State University, May 21, 2014).

'Short Notices', *The English Historical Review*, Vol. 47, No.188 (October 1932).

Smith, Eliza. *The Compleat Housewife* (London, 1729).

Soyer, Alexis. *The Gastronomic Regenerator: A Simplified and Entirely New System of Cookery* (Cambridge: Cambridge University Press, originally published 1846, digitally printed version 2013).

Soyer, Alexis. *A Shilling Cookery for the People* (London: Routledge, 1854).

Spiller, Elizabeth. *Science, Reading and Renaissance Literature: The Art of Making Knowledge, 1580-1670* (Cambridge: Cambridge University Press, 2004).

Spurling, Hilary. *Elinor Fettiplace's Receipt Book* (London: Viking Salamander, 1986).

Stapley, Christina (ed.). *The Receipt Book of Lady Anne Blencowe* (Basingstoke: Heartsease Books, 2004).

von Drachenfels, Suzanne. *The Art of the Table: A Complete Guide to Table Setting, Table Manners and Tableware* (New York, Simon & Schuster, 2000).

Woolley, Hannah. *The Accomplish'd Lady's Delight in Preserving, Physick, Beautifying, and Cookery*, Second edition enlarged (London: B. Harris, 1677).

Woolley, Hannah. *The Cooks Guide: Or, Rare Receipts for Cookery* (London, 1664).

Woolley, Hannah. *The Gentlewoman's Companion or, a Guide to the Female Sex*, with an introduction by Caterina Albano (London, Prospect Books, 2001).

Zapp, Karl-Heinz. 'Ammonium Compounds' in *Ullmann's Encyclopedia of Industrial Chemistry* (Weinheim: Wiley-VCH, 2012).

Online sources

'A Look at Health and Sickness in Upper Swaledale and Arkengarthdale (2017)', by Jocelyn M. Campbell <https://swaag.org/pdf/DalesHealth-JocelynCampbell.pdf>.

'Acton, Eliza (1799-1859)', by Elizabeth Ray, *Oxford Dictionary of National Biography* <https://doi.org/10.1093/ref:odnb/73>.

'Alfred Bird: Egg-free custard inventor and chemist', Birmingham Mail <https://www.birminghammail.co.uk/incoming/alfred-bird-egg-free-custard-inventor-8040314> Retrieved 25 February 2018.

'Beeton [née Mayson], Isabella Mary (1836-1865)', *Oxford Dictionary of National Biography* <https://doi.org/10.1093/ref:odnb/37172>.

'Bertie, Willoughby, fourth earl of Abingdon (1740-1799)' by William C. Lowe, *Oxford Dictionary of National Biography* <https://doi.org/10.1093/ref:odnb/2280>.

'Blaenclydach Boys and the Chocolate Potato Biscuits', by Tony Peters, Glamorgan Archives <https://glamarchives.wordpress.com/2015/05/06/blaenclydach-boys-and-the-chocolate-potato-biscuits/>.

'Block Gingerbread', Food History Jottings, a blog by Ivan Day <http://foodhistorjottings.

blogspot.com/2013/07/block-gingerbread.html>.

'Brummell, George Bryan [known as Beau Brummell] (1778-1840)', by Philip Carter, *Oxford Dictionary of National Biography* <https://doi.org/10.1093/ref:odnb/3771>.

'Chicory on Phillip Island', Australian Food History Timeline <https://australianfoodtimeline.com.au/1870-chicory-on-phillip-island/>.

'Discovering Chocolate: The Great Chocolate Discovery', Cadbury <https://www.cadbury.com.au/about-chocolate/discovering-chocolate.aspx>.

'Furness, Christopher, first Baron Furness (1852-1912)', Gordon Boyce, *Oxford Dictionary of National Biography* <https://doi.org/10.1093/ref:odnb/33295>.

'Glasse [née Allgood], Hannah', by A. H. T. Robb-Smith, *Oxford Dictionary of National Biography* < https://doi.org/10.1093/ref:odnb/10804>.

'Grantley Hall History, Part Two: The Furness Family', Grantley Hall <https://www.grantleyhall.co.uk/news/grantley-hall-history,-part-two--the-furness-family/56-6/>.

'How to bake a First World War Trench cake', *The Telegraph*, 18 August 2018 < https://www.telegraph.co.uk/history/world-war-one/10905975/How-to-bake-a-First-World-War-trench-cake.html>.

'Japanese Garden at Grantley Hall', Historic England <https://historicengland.org.uk/listing/the-list/list-entry/1442593>.

'Potential Toxic Levels of Cyanide in Almonds (*Prunus amygdalus*), Apricot Kernels (*Prunus armeniaca*), and Almond Syrup', by Nadia Chaouali, et al. in *ISRN Toxicology*, 19 September 2013. <https://www.hindawi.com/journals/isrn/2013/610648/>.

'Raffald [née Whitaker] Elizabeth' Nancy Cox, *Oxford Dictionary of National Biography* < https://doi.org/10.1093/ref:odnb/23008>.

'Soyer, Alexis Benoît (1810–1858)', by Elizabeth Ray, *Oxford Dictionary of National Biography* (Oxford: OUP, 2004) <https://doi.org/10.1093/ref:odnb/26076>.

'Springerle, Germany 14th Century', Sweet Tooth Design <https://www.sweetoothdesign.com/cookie-springerle>.

'Stephen Furness', The Peerage <http://www.thepeerage.com/p41556.htm#i415559>.

'Tea-Table Talk: a woman's letter to women', *Cardiff Times and South Wales Weekly News*, Saturday 30 October, 1891 <https://blog.britishnewspaperarchive.co.uk/2017/03/23/cookery-corner-cakes/>.

'Thynne, William', Sidney Lee, revised by A.S.G. Edwards, *Oxford Dictionary of National Biography*, <https://doi.org/10.1093/ref:odnb/27426>.

'Tragacanth', Colony Gums <htpp:www.colonygums.com/tragacanth>.

'White, Gilbert (1720-1793)', by Paul Foster, *Oxford Dictionary of National Biography* <https://doi.org/10.1093/ref:odnb/29243>.

Recipe Index

RECIPE INDEX